Developing Memory Skills in the Primary Classroom

How can we help children to develop their working memory?

The memory demands in the classroom for children are high; they are constantly bombarded by new knowledge in multiple topic areas, given series of instructions to complete and expected to both learn and demonstrate their mastery of knowledge and skills on a daily basis. *Developing Memory Skills in the Primary Classroom* is a highly practical book that contains all the guidance and resources a school needs to boost their pupils' working memory. Proven to have a positive impact on pupils, this tried and tested complete programme combines teaching pupils memory strategies with opportunities to practise those strategies within a small group, the classroom and at home. The resources provided by this book include:

- a variety of photocopiable games and activities
- extensive teaching notes
- a range of sample letters to parents/carers
- essential information sheets
- bespoke baseline assessment tools
- a detailed programme that can be run by a teaching assistant under the guidance of the SENCo.

This text provides a clear link between working in the classroom and with parents in the home, making it a one-stop resource for any teacher, SENCo, teaching assistant or parent wanting to help children develop their working memory.

Gill Davies is a practising teacher and SENCo. She is a Leading SENCo for Nasen delivering their training on using a whole school approach to improving access, participation and achievement.

nasen
Helping Everyone Achieve ■■■

nasen is a professional membership association that supports all those who work with or care for children and young people with special and additional educational needs. Members include teachers, teaching assistants, support workers, other educationalists, students and parents.

nasen supports its members through policy documents, journals, its magazine Special!, publications, professional development courses, regional networks and newsletters. Its website contains more current information such as responses to government consultations. nasen's published documents are held in very high regard both in the UK and internationally.

Other titles published in association with the National Association for Special Educational Needs (nasen):

Language for Learning in the Secondary School: A Practical Guide for Supporting Students with Speech, Language and Communication Needs
Sue Hayden and Emma Jordan
2012/pb: 978-0-415-61975-2

Using Playful Practice to Communicate with Special Children
Margaret Corke
2012/pb: 978-0-415-68767-6

The Equality Act for Educational Professionals: A simple guide to disability and inclusion in schools
Geraldine Hills
2012/pb: 978-0-415-68768-3

More Trouble with Maths: A teacher's complete guide to identifying and diagnosing mathematical difficulties
Steve Chinn
2012/pb: 978-0-415-67013-5

Dyslexia and Inclusion: Classroom Approaches for Assessment, Teaching and Learning, second edition
Gavin Reid
2012/pb: 978-0-415-60758-2

Promoting and Delivering School-to-School Support for Special Educational Needs: A practical guide for SENCOs
Rita Cheminais
2013/pb 978-0-415-63370-3

Time to Talk: Implementing outstanding practice in speech, language and communication
Jean Gross
2013/pb: 978-0-415-63334-5

Assessing Children with Specific Learning Difficulties: A Teacher's Practical Guide
Gavin Reid, Gad Elbeheri and John Everatt
2016/pb: 978-0-415-67027-2

Supporting Children with Down's Syndrome, second edition
Lisa Bentley, Ruth Dance and Elizabeth Morling
2016/pb: 978-1-138-91485-8

Provision Mapping and the SEND Code of Practice: Making it work in primary, secondary and special schools, second edition
Anne Massey
2016/pb: 978-1-138-90707-2

Supporting Children with Medical Conditions, second edition
Susan Coulter, Lesley Kynman, Elizabeth Morling, Rob Grayson and Jill Wing
2016/pb: 978-1-13-891491-9

Achieving Outstanding Classroom Support in Your Secondary School: Tried and tested strategies for teachers and SENCOs
Jill Morgan, Cheryl Jones, Sioned Booth-Coates
2016/pb: 978-1-138-83373-9

Developing Memory Skills in the Primary Classroom

A complete programme for all

Gill Davies

Routledge
Taylor & Francis Group

LONDON AND NEW YORK

Helping Everyone Achieve

First published 2015
by Routledge
2 Park Square, Milton Park, Abingdon, Oxon OX14 4RN

and by Routledge
711 Third Avenue, New York, NY 10017

Routledge is an imprint of the Taylor & Francis Group, an informa business

British Library Cataloguing in Publication Data
A catalogue record for this book is available from the British Library

Library of Congress Cataloging in Publication Data
Davies, Gill.
   Developing memory skills in the primary classroom: a complete programme for all/Gill Davies.
   pages cm
   1. Memory. 2. Memory in children. 3. Education, Primary. I. Title.
   LB1063.D38 2015
   370.15'22–dc23
   2014047226

ISBN: 978-1-138-89261-3 (hbk)
ISBN: 978-1-138-89262-0 (pbk)
ISBN: 978-1-315-70907-9 (ebk)

Typeset in Sabon and Gill Sans
by Florence Production Ltd, Stoodleigh, Devon, UK

Printed and bound in Great Britain by CPI Group (UK) Ltd, Croydon, CR0 4YY

Contents

Preface

I did not plan to write a book about memory difficulties. I set out to create a programme that would meet a need that I had identified in my schools. As the SENCo in two small rural primary schools, I was identifying more and more children whose progress in school was being affected by memory difficulties, and so I looked for a programme that I could use to support them. While I could find books of memory games designed for use with children and books aimed at adults teaching strategies to support memory, there was nothing that combined these two. If a child is struggling in school with an area of numeracy, no teacher would simply give a child more and more maths problems to do and expect them to improve their mathematical skills. Every teacher would give them strategies to help to develop their understanding. Why then would we expect that playing more and more memory games, without being given strategies to support their memory, would be an effective way of helping to improve children's memory skills? Surely children who are struggling with remembering need to be helped to develop strategies to support their memory? Talking to children at school supported this idea. Children who had been identified with memory difficulties were far less likely to be able to explain how they had just tried to remember a certain piece of information, while their peers without memory difficulties more often had a strategy that they used and also an awareness of what this strategy was and the ability to verbalise (with differing levels of success) what they had done.

When you consider that surveys put the number of children who have memory difficulties at 10 per cent (Alloway *et al.*, 2009), the importance of reducing the impact of these difficulties in everyday classroom life, and of helping these pupils to develop an awareness of the strategies that they can use to support themselves, can be seen. Through a combination of monitoring and reducing the memory load placed upon children in the classroom and helping them to develop personal strategies to support their memory, it is possible to reduce the impact of working memory difficulties on children's progress in the classroom. The importance of helping pupils to develop strategies has been shown in research that demonstrates that supporting pupils with an IEP (Individual Educational Plan) or equivalent support is not enough to help pupils with these difficulties catch up with their peers; we must develop their ability to remember and manage information – their working memory (Alloway, 2009).

The memory demands in the classroom for children are high; they are constantly bombarded by new knowledge in multiple topic areas, given series of instructions to complete and expected to both learn and demonstrate their mastery of knowledge and skills on a daily basis. An effective and efficient memory is crucial for success in this system. For example, they may understand a three-step instruction that they have been given, but forget the second and third steps while completing the first. When they are reading a paragraph they may forget what was at the beginning of the paragraph by the time they have reached the end. They will then look like they have a difficulty with comprehension; however, this comprehension difficulty is caused by a failure of their memory system and not their language skills. If they are trying to solve a maths problem that has several steps they may forget where they are in the series of steps while they are trying to solve the problem.

Efforts to support pupils' working memory will also enhance their self-esteem as they will experience more success. When pupils learn to work through a task systematically and have strategies to use to support their memory, classroom tasks will feel less overwhelming, and when we feel calm it is actually easier to get through the work we have been given; that is the aim of this programme.

Chapter 1

Working memory

This chapter looks at:

- the difference between short-term memory, working memory and long-term memory;
- the impact that working memory has on learning;
- the identification of working-memory difficulties.

Types of memory

Memory is our ability to encode, store and subsequently recall information and past experiences. It is the process by which we store knowledge and skills, to be recalled and put to use at a later date.

There are three types of memory; long term, short term and working memory. There has been some confusion between the three types and their exact nature and interrelationship. While the differences between long and short-term memory are clear, the differences between short-term and working memory are less clear cut and there has been some confusion over the use of the two terms.

Long-term memory

Long-term memory is the ability to remember past experiences and skills and is the process of recalling to mind previously learned facts, experiences, impressions, skills and habits. Long-term memory enables the use of past experience to influence our current behaviour. It gives us the capacity to learn and adapt from previous experiences as well as to build relationships. Retrieval of information from long-term memory is aided by meaning and pattern also helps to aid recall by reducing the demands of limited capacity within long-term memory stores.

Short-term memory

Short-term memory is the temporary storage of information. Short-term memory has a more limited capacity.

Working memory

Working memory is a key cognitive function that is used in daily life to hold information. It involves short-term storage and manipulation of information in order to complete a task. Working memory can be distinguished from short-term memory as it involves both storage and processing of information. Working memory is the system that underlies the ability to store and manipulate information over a short period of time. It functions as a mental post-it note for information and has several interacting subsystems to store verbal and visual-spatial information and attention control. It is a useful and flexible mental working space, however, it can also be very fragile. It has several important characteristics:

1   Working memory has a limited capacity; trying to hold too much information leads to memory failure.
2   Information is rapidly lost from the working memory when attention is turned away from it, either due to internal or external distractions.
3   Overload or distraction leads to information being irretrievably lost from working memory.
4   Working memory has been shown to be necessary for the control of attention and to resist distractions. Working memory and the control of attention are inseparable (Klingberg, 2009).

Working memory is used every day; socially, academically and professionally. While working memory develops during childhood and adulthood reaching maximum capacity at about 30 years, it then gradually declines with age. The average adult cannot hold more than 6–7 units of information in their short-term memory, however there is substantial variation in working memory capacity between individuals.

While we know that the size of an individual's working memory can vary greatly, it is currently not fully understood what causes this variation. It is known that poor working memory is not strongly related to factors relating to a person's background, or quality of life experiences or educational experience. It has been shown that working memory is a better predictor of success in the classroom in subjects as varied as language, maths, history and art (Cowan and Alloway, 2008). In the average class the class teacher copes with a range of latent ability, but they also need to be aware that they will have a similar range of working memory capacity. For example, in a typical class of Y3 children, the working memory capacities will probably range from those of the average 4-year-old to those of the average 11-year-old. These differences will impact on their ability to cope with classroom activities. Living with working memory difficulties can be compared to working with an old computer – slow, frustrating and very inefficient.

Children at school use their working memory on a daily basis for a variety of tasks, for example, following instructions or remembering their place in the sentence they are writing. Working memory is essential for many classroom activities including mental arithmetic, reading comprehension and copying from the board. Since children are often required to hold information in mind while engaged in other activities, working memory is vital for many learning activities in the classroom. Children with small working memory will fail in these tasks simply because they cannot hold sufficient information in their heads to enable them to complete the task.

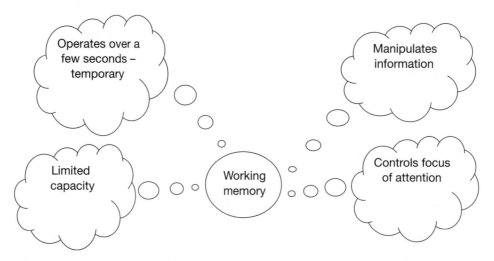

Figure 1.1 The key characteristics of working memory

The impact of working-memory difficulties

Working memory and learning are inseparable. The importance of working memory in learning cannot be underestimated as it is a core cognitive process and predicts academic learning. Learning involves acquiring new knowledge and skills, however, it is vital to remember and retain what we have learned if we are to be able to use it again and memory is the process by which we achieve this. Learning is a step-by-step process, based on the success of successive learning tasks.

Working memory difficulties can have a wide-ranging impact on pupils. Most pupils with working memory difficulties will experience some difficulties in the classroom. A wide range of research has shown that the majority of pupils with memory difficulties will be slow to learn in the areas of reading, maths and science, across both the primary and secondary school years (Gathercole and Alloway, 2008). Conversely, children with high working memory scores typically show excellent reading skills at all ages and do very well in maths (Gathercole and Alloway, 2008). It has been suggested that children with working memory difficulties are unable to meet the memory demands of many structured learning activities. Gathercole and Alloway (2008) argue that as a result the memory becomes overloaded and the crucial information that is needed to guide an ongoing activity is permanently lost. It is then not possible for the child to successfully complete the activity unless they are able to access this information and so the child either guesses the next step or abandons their task. This is then a missed learning opportunity for the child and a series of these misses can result in gaps in a child's learning; the more frequent the gaps, the more the learning will be delayed. Children with working memory difficulties fail in many different activities on many occasions, and so they will struggle to achieve normal rates of learning and tend to make poor academic progress.

The majority of studies suggest that children who are having difficulties in maths have memory deficits (Swanson and Jerman, 2006). Memory deficits affect mathematical performance in several ways:

- Performance with simple arithmetic depends on speedy and efficient retrieval from long-term memory.
- The temporary storage of numbers when working out the answer to a mathematical problem is crucial. Working memory difficulties make problem-solving extremely difficult.
- Poor recall of facts from memory increases the cognitive demands of a task as they then have to be calculated and this leads to difficulties in problem-solving strategies.

Research also shows that maths disabilities are frequently co-morbid with reading disabilities (Swanson and Jerman, 2006). Students with co-occurring maths and reading disabilities fall further behind in maths achievement than those with only a maths disability. However, research shows that the most common deficit among all students with a maths disability, with or without a co-occurring reading disability, is a difficulty in performing with working-memory tasks.

From this it can be seen that early identification and support of children with working memory is vital if we are to be able to avoid underachievement. Early identification will mean that teachers are able to adapt their teaching methods before children start to fall too far behind their peers.

In some cases, interventions can place high demands on memory and make learning more difficult rather than alleviating difficulties. It is essential that the teacher considers the memory demands of any strategies they are using with children and adapts the approach that they are using if the memory demands of the task are high.

Working memory also has a central role in our personal organisation; in order to be organised we carry around a mental list of what we need to do throughout the day. If this list is quickly lost from memory, keeping track of what has been done and what is left to do is a difficult task. Many children with working-memory difficulties present as being poorly organised.

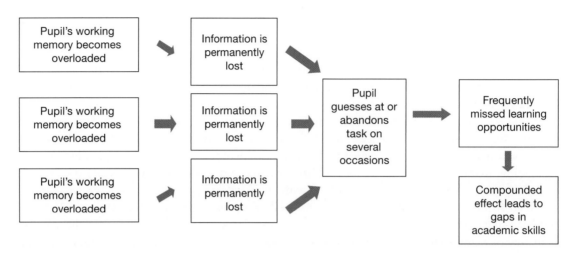

Figure 1.2 How does working memory lead to reduced academic success?

How can working-memory difficulties be identified?

The first step in being able to support children with working-memory difficulties is to be able to identify who these children are. Working-memory difficulties are often mistaken for a lack of motivation or concentration.

A checklist of these characteristics is included in the photocopiable resources for teachers to use as a means of identifying those children that may have memory difficulties.

Poor organisational skills/attention and concentration difficulties

A child with these characteristics:

- fails to follow multi-step instructions;
- tends to lose their belongings;
- has difficulty keeping their place in a complex task with multiple steps;
- struggles with activities that combine storing and processing information;
- has difficulty maintaining attention and staying on task;
- appears to be lacking in motivation;
- appears to be inattentive;
- is easily distracted, especially when working on something that is not of interest to them;
- shows poor attention to detail;
- has difficulty getting started on a piece of work;
- has difficulty when planning something that needs to be done in separate steps;
- has difficulty in integrating new information with prior knowledge;
- when chosen to answer a question forgets what he/she wanted to say;
- has difficulty staying on task when tasks are cognitively demanding, but attends well when cognitive demands of the task are minimal;
- has trouble waiting his/her turn; for example, in a conversation or when asking for help;
- benefits from teacher support to stay on task and complete longer tasks;
- does not carry out classroom instructions accurately, i.e. will complete some but not all steps of an instruction;
- forgets how to continue an activity that they have started;
- is unable to explain what they should be doing during an activity.

Difficulties in literacy

A child with these characteristics:

- has difficulty remembering a story in sequence;
- has difficulty remembering their place in a sentence or paragraph they are writing;
- has difficulty in understanding and following a story they are reading;
- has difficulty in remembering grammatical rules;
- has difficulty in note-taking or copying from the board;
- has difficulty taking notes and listening at the same time;
- makes poor progress in literacy.

Difficulties in numeracy

A child with these characteristics:

- is inconsistent in remembering maths facts;
- has difficulty in learning and retrieving mathematical facts and applying them in problem solving;
- has difficulty remembering a sequence of four or more numbers;
- has difficulty with problems that require holding information in mind, for example, mental maths calculations;
- exhibits slow information retrieval;
- has difficulty learning mathematical procedures;
- makes poor progress in numeracy.

Figure 1.3 The characteristics of a child with working-memory difficulties

Chapter 2

Classroom strategies to support memory

This chapter looks at:

- general strategies to support pupils with memory difficulties in the classroom;
- strategies for literacy;
- strategies for numeracy.

Classroom support for working-memory difficulties involves teachers managing pupils' working-memory loads with the aim of reducing the negative impact of excessive memory loads. If we can prevent this overload from causing the loss of crucial information from the working memory, the pupils have a better chance of being able to complete their tasks.

Working-memory deficits have a large impact on the learning within classrooms. In recent years, there has been a push to make classrooms dyslexia-friendly and in just the same way, an increased awareness on the part of teachers can make a classroom memory-supportive. In just the same way as the dyslexia-friendly classrooms benefit all learners, all learners will benefit from strategies to support memory when they are introduced into everyday classroom practice. In general, when teachers use simple, clear, chunked instructions and reduce memory loads, pupil attention and achievement will increase for all pupils, not just those with memory difficulties.

Teachers have been working to make lessons multi-sensory for some time, and this is important for pupils' different memory preferences. Each pupil will learn best in their own way (whether the pupil is aware of which strategies suit their style of learning or not). When information is presented in a variety of formats the teacher increases the probability of reaching a larger proportion of pupils in the class. The use of memory strategies can help pupils to increase their ability to organise and recall information and so enhance their ability to remember.

!	Remembering sequences of three or more unrelated words or numbers	!	Following long or complex instructions
!	Writing a long sentence containing detail/facts	!	Keeping track of the place you have reached in a complex task with many steps

Figure 2.1 Tasks with high memory loads

A key factor in a pupil's success in a task is their ability to follow, understand and remember instructions. There are simple steps that teachers can take to make instructions clearer and more accessible to pupils with memory difficulties.

Modifying instructions within lessons to reduce working-memory loads will benefit all pupils not just those with memory difficulties. Areas to consider are:

- Using shorter sentences or reducing the number of steps in instructions. Always give instructions in the sequence in which the actions should be done.
- Keep the grammar of the sentences simple.
- Break down complex tasks into a series of smaller tasks and only give instructions for each part of the sequence as the pupil is ready.
- Provide task planners to act as a memory aid for more complex tasks.

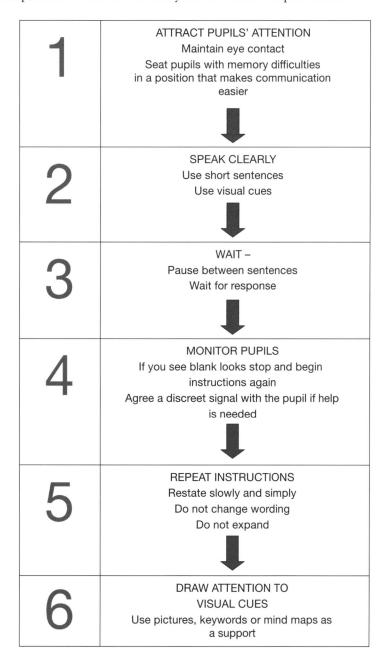

Figure 2.2 Flow chart for helping pupils to process instructions in the classroom

Comprehension is key; it is much more challenging to remember something that you do not fully understand. Making connections between old and new learning helps this. The better you can link new learning to something the children already know, the better they will remember it.

Talk is powerful in the classroom both for supporting comprehension and memory; encourage pupils to talk about the topics they are trying to learn – to anyone who will listen!

1. Monitor the child	• Watch for warning signs in behaviour. • Ask the child about difficulties – verbally check understanding of instructions or devise a hand signal for the child to use when they need help. • Ask the child to verbalise the steps in completing tasks they often struggle to complete; this may indicate where the breakdown is occurring. Support can then be provided at the appropriate point.
2. Recognise working memory failures	• Look for warning signs – incomplete recall, failure to following instructions, abandoning tasks, losing their place (e.g. pupil cannot remember the words in the sentence they are trying to write). • Remember that anxiety reduces listening ability.
3. Evaluate working memory loads	• Causes of heavy workloads – long sequences, unfamiliar content and activities with demanding mental processing. • Pupils with memory difficulties will need more support for longer, more complex tasks that have unfamiliar content or more complex mental processing.
4. Reduce working memory loads	• Reduce amount to be remembered. • Break complex tasks into smaller chunks. • Keep instructions concise, clear and to the point. • Simplify the structures of speech. • Repeat instructions without changing wording. • Provide written instructions or task plans for reference. • Increase familiarity of content. • Make content meaningful to the pupil by providing examples that the pupil can relate to, or linking information to be remembered, i.e. using pattern and meaningful association (e.g. mum, dad, son is easier to remember than table, cat and bike). • Provide information in multiple ways; speak it, show it, physically work with it or model it.
5. Be aware that as processing demands increase working memory loads increase (for example, identifying and blending individual sounds in words where there are more than two phonemes is demanding for pupils with working memory difficulties)	• Simplify mental processing. • Modify the learning activity to reduce the amount to be remembered. • Reduce amount of mental processing by providing clues, e.g. give key words so that the student does not have to remember everything. • Develop routines (e.g. for collecting equipment needed to start maths lessons). Once a routine becomes automatic it does not require conscious thought and reduces working memory demand. • Allow extra time for pupils to retrieve information.

Figure 2.3 Steps for a memory supportive classroom

6. Repeat and review frequently	• Be prepared to repeat key information frequently. • Pause at least twice in a lesson and ask pupils to summarise what they have learnt so far and draw/write on the board to record this information. Listening to other pupils repeat key points can be valuable for all the children. • Ask pupils to repeat back verbal instructions to the class. • Use teachers, TAs and fellow pupils to provide repetition. • Use task plans and breakdowns to repeat key information (however, just making these available is not sufficient to guarantee their use; give opportunities for pupils to practise and develop the skill of using these tools). • Provide opportunities to repeat tasks. • Encourage pupils to practise information to be remembered in several short sessions that are repeated during the day. A few minutes two or three times a day will be more effective than one long session.
7. Encourage the use of memory aids	• Use working walls, wall charts, posters, personalised dictionaries, cubes, counters, mind maps, number lines, multiplication grids, memory cards, audio recorders, computer software.
8. Develop self-awareness of strategies	• Asking for help or repetition when they cannot remember. • Using rehearsal, visualisation, chunking, etc. • Developing note taking. • Use of long-term memory. • Organisational strategies. • Discuss possible strategies to increase pupils' awareness of the different strategies and how effective they are for different tasks.

Figure 2.3 Continued

As well as considering the clarity of the communication in the classroom for all pupils, there are other considerations that can support pupils with working memory difficulties.

If you have detected a particular area of difficulty for a child, there are different strategies that can be put into place to provide support.

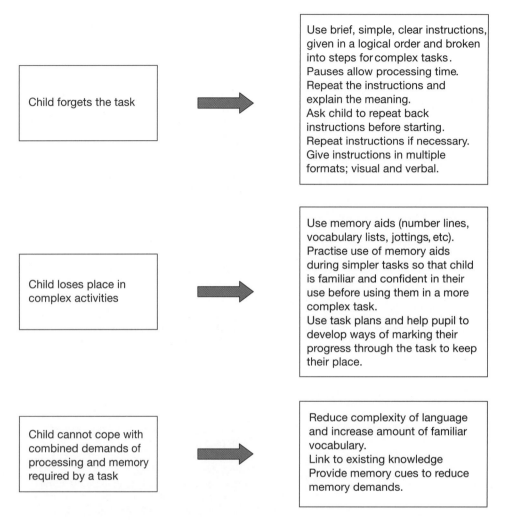

Figure 2.4 Problems and solutions for memory difficulties in the classroom

Strategies for literacy

The following strategies are useful for literacy.

- Avoid asking pupils to copy from the board.
- Allow alternative methods of recording (mind maps, diagrams, dictaphones).
- Use dictaphones for children to temporarily record their sentences and use as a personal support for writing (replaying it to themselves as they write the sentence to reduce the memory demands of the task).
- Reading comprehension is greatly impacted by working memory difficulties. A reader needs to hold the words decoded in print for enough time to link them together and produce a meaningful sentence and then link this sentence to the next to form a coherent paragraph. Comprehension difficulties are increased if the reader also has difficulties decoding and blending the individual words, as this increases the cognitive demands of the task and contributes to memory overload. Teaching pupils active reading skills can help with this; highlight keywords and jot down main ideas, identify keywords relating to inference and link these to the main keywords. Give the pupil a photocopy of the pages they are working on so

that they can highlight keywords and draw pictures and make notes around the page to annotate the text and support their memory and so aid comprehension. Pupils can then go back and reread their jottings/highlighted words in the text to consolidate the information in their memory.

- Prepare the pupils' memory before reading/listening; cues that prepare pupils for the task they have been given can reduce the memory load. Giving the pupils comprehension questions to answer and listen out for before starting to read a story aloud or explain a concept to the class can help them to focus on key pieces of information. The same strategy can be useful for students to use when they are working independently on a reading comprehension; reading the first couple of questions before reading the text will help them to focus on the salient information they need to find to answer the questions.
- Teaching onset and rime is important for reducing the memory demands of phonetic decoding. Words can then be decoded by analogy rather than decoding each word phoneme by phoneme. In this way, lists such as dog, log, fog, hog, bog, etc. can be decoded by just changing the initial sound.
- Using dictation sentences is a good way to practise and test spellings. It also helps pupils to transfer their learning from weekly spelling lists and apply them in their writing.
- Use pictures and visuals to support learning; for example, pupils can draw pictures of homophones like hare and hair, hear and here.

1 Dictate whole sentence
2 Ask the pupil to repeat it back to you
3 Dictate it again saying each word clearly, in smaller chunks if necessary to reduce working memory load
4 Pupil writes each sentence chunk, saying the words aloud as he/she writes them
5 Pupil is asked to read back exactly what they have written
6 Final corrections are made if they are needed

Figure 2.5 Strategy for spelling sentence dictation

Strategies for numeracy

The following strategies are useful for numeracy.

1 Teach jotting strategies to reduce working-memory loads during mental maths tasks (whiteboards are good for this).
2 Teach the children to write down the steps involved when working on a word problem. This will prevent them from losing their place and forgetting what they are doing.
3 Make resources readily available to pupils so that they are able to work with practical resources when calculating.
4 Stick a numberline (1–100) to the table surface for frequent reference.
5 If pupils are using fingers to support their calculations encourage them to touch each finger on their chin as they count so that they know which ones have been counted.

Strategies for foundation subjects

The following strategies are useful for foundation subjects:

1   using diagrams to help pupils see and organise what they are trying to learn;

  - venn diagrams for comparing and contrasting;
  - topic web for main ideas;
  - cause and effect box – the event goes in a middle box with the causes listed in boxes to the right with arrows going to the event and the effects are listed in boxes to the left;

2   using storytelling to remember the main points of information for any topic, especially if events need to be remembered in a specific sequence.

Chapter 3

The memory programme
The importance of measuring impact

This chapter looks at:

- data from use of the programme;
- baseline measures;
- factors the increase the impact of the programme.

Although working memory has been studied for decades, it has only recently been proved to be a 'plastic' function of the brain (Klingberg, 2009) that can be strengthen by training. This finding gives support for developing a programme to help children strengthen their memory skills.

Any intervention needs to include a baseline so that its impact can be evaluated. This is important both from the point of view of the impact that the programme is having on the individual pupils and also in terms of staff accountability for the use of time and resources. Measurements of the impact of a programme can be used both to justify the time and resources expended on them and also to adapt and tailor the programme to the individual pupils so that they gain the maximum benefit from them.

While it is possible to buy commercially produced assessments for working memory that will provide standardised scores, they tend to have a high cost and school budgets are limited. The baseline measure included here has been successfully used to monitor the impact of this programme over the past four years and while it does not give you standardised scores it does enable you to measure individual children's performance before and after the programme and so measure impact of the programme on their memory skills.

Data from use of the programme in schools shows that while the amount of increase in the baseline score varies from pupil to pupil, every pupil made some gains. The baseline assessment is scored out of 100.

	Baseline score	Post intervention score	Gain
Range of scores	10–21	21–59	11–28
Average score	14.2	37.3	17.6

Figure 3.1 Baseline data

Factors increasing the impact of the programme

The following factors appear to be linked both to greater increases in pupil baseline scores and subjective reports from class teachers of pupils' increased use of strategies in the classroom.

- Short regular sessions – three times a week.
- Parental engagement to encourage the use of strategies outside school in everyday situations.

- Class teachers who are engaged with the use of the programme and the strategies, who encourage pupils to share the strategies learned in sessions with the rest of the class and make reference to them during class lessons.
- Strategy reminder posters added to the classroom wall as the different strategies are covered in a visible position.

Baseline assessment

This should be carried out individually with each child before starting the programme. It will enable you to see any individual strengths and weaknesses and to measure the impact of the programme. The assessment is challenging and pupils are not expected to attain a high score in the assessment before the programme. It is important that this is the case, as if a pupil scored 9/10 before the programme there would be little potential for showing improvement. Whereas, an initial score of 2/10 gives plenty of room for improvement. Photocopiable recording and resource sheets are contained in the photocopiable resources section.

Baseline assessment tasks

1   Listen to the numbers that I call out – can you repeat the sequence back to me? The sequences will increase in length.
2   Listen to the numbers that I call out – can you repeat the sequence back to me in the reverse order, i.e. give me the last number first? The sequences will increase in length.
3   Study the card with 20 pictures on it for 30 seconds. Cover the sheet. How many can you remember in any order?
4   Look at the card with a line of 10 digits on it for 30 seconds. How many of the numbers can you remember in the correct order?
5   Look at the card with a line of 10 shapes on it for 30 seconds. How many of the numbers can you remember in the correct order?
6   Listen to the list of colours I give you, then turn over your page and colour the strip of boxes in those colours in the same order that you heard them.

red	yellow	green	blue	orange
blue	yellow	red	black	purple
orange	green	yellow	blue	black
purple	green	blue	red	yellow

Figure 3.2 Colours to tell the children

Before starting to use this with the children, use felt tips or coloured pencils to colour the grid squares as labelled.

7   Look at the grid and study the position of the different coloured squares for 30 seconds. Can you colour the squares in the same pattern on the blank grid?
8   Look at the grid and try to remember the position of the dots. Cover the grid and try to draw the dots on the blank copy.

Evaluative assessment

At the end of the course it is important to re-run the baseline assessment in exactly the same way as at the beginning so that you can evaluate the progress that the children have made and the effectiveness of the course.

Chapter 4

The memory programme
Getting started

This chapter looks at:

- the aims and objectives of the programme;
- how to run a memory club;
- the structure of regular sessions;
- the importance of learning to listen;
- the introductory and learning-to-listen sessions.

Aims of the programme

The aims are:

- to enable the children to maximise their short-term memory by acquiring and implementing memory strategies;
- to support the children in applying the strategies learned in the group to both classroom activities and in their lives outside school.

Objectives of intervention

The aim is that children:

1   have a simple understanding of short-term and long-term memory, and how we use them;
2   acquire and deploy memory strategies successfully;
3   maximise their memory capacity by implementing these strategies both in and out of the intervention sessions (using naming, rehearsing, visualisation, linking, chunking and grouping);
4   can enhance their confidence and self-esteem.

A sample memory club session

How to run a memory club

It is important to teach one strategy at a time in focused sessions and allow opportunity to practise each strategy. Teach students when, where, why and how to use the strategy outside the sessions. Include the following steps in teaching a strategy:

1   use clear, direct language;
2   model strategies and think aloud;
3   review prior knowledge; how is this like/different from another strategy;
4   encourage the use of (and practise using) activities in the programme;

5   evaluate and recognise success and effort;
6   encourage children's awareness of which strategies suit their personal learning style;
7   discuss the situations/tasks for which each new strategy may be useful;
8   promote transfer to classroom and home using memory aid posters, letters home to parents and classroom discussion of which strategies may be useful during a given task.

It is important that the memory club has a regular routine and structure to the sessions; this reduces the memory demands of the sessions as it helps the children know what to expect.

Involving parents

Before beginning the sessions ensure that each child has taken home and returned to school the permission slip on the bottom of the parent consent letter (see the Resources chapter). The advice sheets for parents should also be sent home throughout the course as each new strategy is covered. Parents should be kept informed of the strategies that the children have learned so that they can then encourage them to use them at home when they need to remember something.

Structure

Below is a sample structure for a memory club.

1   Warm-up activity: every session should start with a warm-up activity to focus the children and settle them to work. Chose one of the games from the previous session and repeat it as the warm-up. This will also serve to reinforce the work from the previous session.
2   Memory club posters: go through the reminder posters together and use these to recap the memory techniques you have covered so far.
3   Main activities for the session: this will either be continuing to work on the same technique as the previous session (providing a chance to revisit and apply the strategy) or introducing a new technique. Before and after each activity it is important to explicitly discuss with the children what memory enhancing technique they are using.
4   Recap the techniques used in the session and consider when these approaches would be useful at home and at school. Remind children that everyone is different, that they will find some techniques more useful than others and they may prefer different techniques from the others in the group. They need to decide what works for them.

A number of games and activities are provided for practising each strategy. It is not expected that each group of children will always complete every activity before moving to a new strategy. Be guided by the children in the group; when you feel they have developed a level of proficiency with the strategy they are working on, move on to the next. It is important not to go too fast – giving the pupils several new strategies before each has become familiar and can confuse rather than help.

Pupils with memory difficulties find following explanations and discussion in the classroom very challenging. Many of them will have started to expect to lose the thread of classroom discussions. If you do not expect to be able to follow and understand something, you are far more likely to give up sooner. This section looks at the importance of making children active participants in the classroom; you cannot remember something that you have not listened to and understood. For this reason sessions on listening skills are included in the programme before the sessions working directly on memory skills.

Introductory session

It is important to start the sessions with one to give the children the understanding of the aims of the course and how it can help them. The main discussion points are listed below.

Why a memory club?

Start with a discussion with the children – what is memory? What does it do? How do we remember? Why do we need to remember things? What things are easy/hard to remember? Why do we forget? Discuss the aims of the intervention group with the children. Share personal examples of when you forget things.

What factors influence memory?

Explore factors that can weaken the performance of memory by asking the children if they have noticed that there are some times when they find it harder to remember things than other times. Factors that influence memory include hunger, dehydration, tiredness, distractions, overload, illness and anxiety. Reassure children that everyone forgets things from time to time and if possible share an example of your own forgetfulness.

What tools can support our memory?

Brainstorm things that grown-ups use to aid memory:

- Physical: for example, calendars, diaries, lists, notes, etc. Discuss school staff/family members that children have seen using memory aids recently.
- Attitude: for example, good observation, listening, concentration, asking others for help, working together, the importance of a positive mindset. Discuss the importance of concentrating on one thing at a time. Demonstrate this to the children by asking them to draw a square in the air with their right hand, keep doing this and looking at their right hand, while they draw circles on a piece of paper with their left without looking at it. What happens to the circles they are drawing?
- Strategies: what is a strategy? How is it different from a memory aid? Explain to the children that a memory aid is a physical tool (e.g. a notebook) but a strategy is how they approach a task and can be used at any time. Explain how different strategies work better for different tasks and that different people find that different strategies work better for them than others. Explain that we will be working on different strategies during these sessions.

Session 1

In order to be able to remember something you must listen/look carefully. If you do not you will not have seen/heard the important information and you will not be able to remember it. It is important to listen for the information carrying words in sentences.

Listening skills

This is a useful task for children to consider how they listen and to help them to realise that listening is an active process involving some effort on the part of the listener.

ACTIVITY 1: LISTEN AND DO

Explain to the group that they have to follow the instructions. It is important for them to carry out the instructions in the order that they are given. The instructions are short in the beginning and they will get longer. They must not move until all the instructions have been given and the word 'go' indicates they can begin.

Remind the children that they need to concentrate and listen carefully to all the instructions. For children who consistently watch the others for cues, it may be helpful to have some individual turns.

Two step instructions

- Touch your head, rub your tummy. Go.
- Clap your hands, wiggle your fingers. Go.
- Put your hands on your head, touch your nose. Go.

After working at this level, stop and ask the group to identify the information-carrying words in some of the instructions, i.e. the keywords that they need to remember. For example, for the instruction 'put your hands on your head' or 'touch your nose', the information-carrying words are 'hands', 'head', 'touch nose'. There is no need to remember the other words and so you have reduced the memory demands of the task. Identifying the keywords to remember is a useful skill and it is helpful to stop regularly and ask the group to identify them from instructions until you are certain they are all able to do this with confidence.

Three step instructions

- Touch your nose, rub your tummy, and touch your shoulders. Go.
- Wave your arms, touch your toes, and clap your hands. Go.
- Lift both hands above your head, nod your head and touch your ears. Go.
- Touch your toes, wave your arms and wiggle your fingers. Go.

Four step instructions

- Stretch, yawn, clap your hands and slap your knees. Go.
- Rub your tummy, touch your toes, say hello and stamp your feet. Go.
- Stick out your tongue, wiggle your fingers, shake your head and shrug your shoulders. Go.
- Hands up, wriggle your fingers, rub your tummy and touch your nose. Go.

Five step instructions

- Touch your head, rub your tummy, clap your hands, wiggle your fingers and touch your nose. Go.
- Put your hands on your head, touch your nose, rub your tummy, and touch your shoulders and wave your arms. Go.
- Touch your toes, clap your hands, lift both hands above your head, nod your head and touch your ears. Go.
- Touch your toes, wave your arms, wiggle your fingers, tap your head and draw circles in the air with both arms. Go.

ACTIVITY 2: COPY ME

Give each child a drum. The teacher beats out a simple rhythm on their drum and the children take it in turns to repeat it. Start with a pattern that is three beats long and if the group are able to repeat it add an extra beat to the next turn. Once the group is achieving success at four beats, add an extra beat. Continue this way adding extra beats as the group are ready.

To give the game an extra dimension the children can take it in turns to give the target rhythm for the whole group, or can work in pairs creating rhythms for each other to repeat.

ACTIVITY 3: LISTEN AND DRAW

Give each child a copy of the listen and draw worksheet (see photocopiable resources). Tell them they that they need to listen carefully to the instructions you give them and draw the things you say in the correct box. It is useful to ask the children to identify the information-carrying words in some of these instructions. Repeating this within different games will help them to transfer this technique to different situations. Start with an example:

1   In the middle of box 1 draw a large tree.
2   Put four apples on the tree.
3   In the top left corner of the box draw a cloud.
4   In the opposite corner draw the sun.

Wait after each instruction until all the children are ready to listen to the next instruction – this activity is about the need to listen carefully NOT about using memory to remember the sequence of instructions. Ask the children to compare their picture with their neighbour's, is it the same? Then continue with the game:

1   In the top corner of box 2 draw a star.
2   In the middle of box 8 draw a cloud.
3   In the middle of box 7 draw a ball.
4   In the top corner of box 3 draw a spider.
5   In the bottom corner of box 4 draw a crown.
6   Put a snake under the ball in box 7.
7   Draw a fish in the middle of the cloud in box 8.
8   Put a big moon and seven small stars in box 5.
9   Put a rainbow in box 6.
10 Draw a big smiley face under the rainbow.

Ask the children to compare their picture with their neighbour's. Are the pictures the same? Are there any differences? Discuss the importance of listening carefully with the children.

Memory club poster 1

An A4 copy of the poster is put up in the room where the group is being held to act as a memory aid. It will help with the transfer of skills between the group, the classroom and home if another copy is put on the classroom wall and children are given a smaller A5 copy to take home. Transfer of skills back to the classroom is also aided by the teacher making explicit reference to the posters and memory strategies during class sessions.

Wherever possible the class teacher should try to encourage the children to extend the use of these strategies from the intervention group to the classroom, by reminding them of the strategies and suggesting which ones would be useful for the current task. As the strategies are covered, the posters that remind the children to use each strategy in the classroom should be put on the classroom wall.

Chapter 5

Introduction to the memory programme
Memory strategies

This chapter looks at:

- naming and rehearsal;
- visualisation;
- keywords for meaning;
- keywords and visualisation;
- visualisation and repetition
- chaining and linking;
- visualisation and linking;
- visual organisers for information;
- chunking.

Strategies to support memory

Using a strategy to support your memory means that you are slowing down the process of remembering and are also engaging conscious effort in the process. This will have a positive impact on the amount you remember. It also gives you the opportunity to quality control the process and evaluate which of the strategies work for you for different tasks. Using strategies enhances pupils' ability to organise and retrieve information, and so can increase the amount that the pupil can recall.

This chapter gives an outline of each memory strategy covered by the memory programme. It would be useful for the class teacher to be aware of the contents of this chapter so that they are able to encourage the use of these strategies in the classroom. Everyone is different, and just as different people have different preferred learning styles they will also have different memory strategies that they feel more comfortable with using and that are more effective for them.

Naming and rehearsal

This technique involves repetition of words, either silently to yourself (rehearsal) or quietly out loud (naming) so that they are more easily remembered. This is useful for remembering telephone numbers, lists of objects you need to go and collect or sequences of tasks that you need to do, etc.

Teachers can help the children to use this task in the class by using short, simple instructions which, once the children have understood them they then reduce to the keywords for the children to repeat, for example, 'colour the pictures, cut them out, sort them into three sets, stick them down' becomes 'colour, cut, sort, stick'.

Counting items

Checking items off on our fingers is helpful as a target to know how many items we need to remember. It can also help to trigger recall. If you have to remember four things but can only remember three, knowing you need one more and going over the task of checking it off on your fingers can act as a trigger to either recall the item or ask for help to remember it.

Using a multi-sensory approach

Encouraging pupils to use a multi-sensory approach when they are using rehearsal to help learn facts by heart can increase the impact of this strategy; say it, read it, write it, sing it, draw it!

Visualisation

Visualisation is using the technique of making mental images to aid memory. It involves making a mental picture in your head so that you can remember it. When we make an internal visual image of information we have heard it helps us to remember it: thinking in colours, pictures and shapes is more memorable than thinking in words. It can be useful in literacy for remembering the main points in a text.

Keywords for meaning

Keywords are the main ideas in a message. When we talk, much of what we say is not needed. For example, 'Look at the time, it's getting late, if we don't hurry we are going to be late for school. Hurry up and go and clean your teeth and brush your hair. Make sure you have put your reading book in your school bag and don't forget your lunchbox.'

In the second version below the keywords are in italics.

Look at the time, it's getting late, if we don't *hurry* we are going to be late for school. Hurry up and go and clean your *teeth* and brush your *hair*. Make sure you have put your *reading book* in your school bag and don't forget your *lunchbox*.

This links back to both rehearsal and visualisation, because it is really only the keywords that need to be rehearsed or visualised. It is only essential that this important information is remembered – anything else is a bonus!

Keywords and visualisation

Combining the techniques of visualisation and looking for keywords can be very effective for some people. Using the skill of finding the keywords to know which objects to put into your mental picture will cut down the amount you are trying to remember. Combining this with using visualisation to help to build up a mental picture of the objects you need to remember is an effective memory strategy.

Visualisation and repetition

Remind the children that they can use more than one strategy at a time to help then to remember. Encourage them to make a visual picture of what they want to remember and also repeat the keywords to themselves.

Chaining and linking

Chaining or linking ideas helps children to remember information because it helps them to group information together. There are several ways in which information can be linked. One way of linking is to use categories, another is to link items together that need to be remembered from different categories using a silly story or picture. Alternatively linking something that you are trying to remember with something that is meaningful to you can be an effective strategy. Many adults use this strategy when trying to remember PIN numbers for cash cards – using relatives' birthdays or phone numbers is a popular way to help recall the number. By doing this you are assigning some information that is meaningful to you, which you can remember, to the information you want to be able to remember. Other useful methods of linking are linking information to a rhythm (like rapping) or putting the words to be remembered to the tune of a well-known song.

Visualisation and linking

This journey system links together the skills of visualisation and association and is useful for remembering a list of information. Start by using a place that is familiar to you. The example below is from my own school and is the route from the classroom furthest away to the staff room. I imagine that I am walking from the classroom to the staff room. I go out of the classroom door, along the landing, down the stairs, turn the corner and go through the double doors, along the corridor past the doors to classes 2 and 1 and through the double door. I go through the cloakroom and along the corridor by the bell rope, past the old front door and through the ICT suite and into the staff room.

Using this route I can remember a series of objects in order by visualising them at particular points on my route, for example:

> You come out of the classroom door, Michael Jackson is standing by the door, on the landing there is a big bunch of red flowers, half way down the stairs there is a chocolate cake and at the bottom of the stairs is a toilet. Turn the corner and go through the double doors: Mickey Mouse holds the doors open for you. Go along the corridor past the door to class 2, in the door way there is a tub of ice cream. Carry on along the corridor, outside class 1 there is a basket of fruit. On the blue double doors there is a monkey, go through the double door and into the cloakroom. In the cloakroom there is large TV. Go through the cloakroom and along the corridor by the bell rope. Under the bell rope there is a plate of cheese sandwiches. Go past the old front door (on the floor by the door is a bucket of milk) and through the ICT suite. On one of the tables there is a packet of chocolate biscuits. Go into the staff room. On the sofa you see David Beckham.

Do this yourself – you will be surprised how many things you can remember in the correct sequence!

Visual organisers for information

There are many different forms in which information can be presented visually, all of which can provide a source of memory support. It is important to remember that these are just as effective if pupils use them by drawing pictures to support their memory as they are if they use words.

Mind maps

Mind maps are another useful visual way of linking information together; providing children with simple scaffolding for them to record either pictures of words that link together to aid their memory. They are useful for providing an overview of a topic.

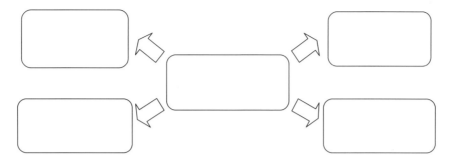

Figure 5.1 An example of a mind map

Venn diagrams

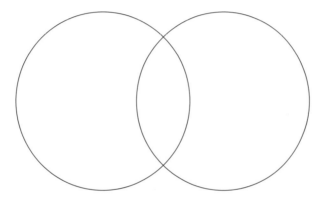

Figure 5.2 An example of a venn diagram

Venn diagrams are useful for displaying information in categories and displaying the similarities and differences between categories.

Sequence diagrams

These are useful for displaying information for which the sequence is important. Charts can either go across or down the page.

Figure 5.3 An example of a sequence organiser

Cause and effect diagram

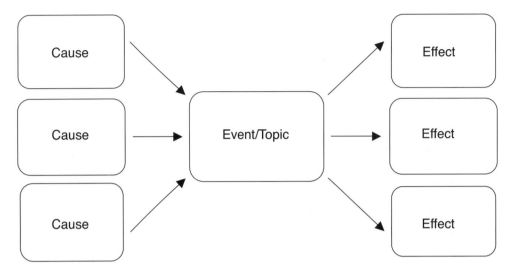

Figure 5.4 An example of a cause and effect chart

The name of the topic is written in the middle box. Causes are listed in the boxes on the left and effects are listed in the boxes on the right.

Chunking

Chunking is where information is broken down into smaller parts that are easier to retain. For example, when we say telephone numbers we automatically chunk them into sections; 01635219742 is difficult to remember as one long number, it is longer than the seven digits that most people can hold in their short-term memory. However, divided into 01635 219 742, most people will find it much easier to remember. Chunking can be used for:

- remembering vocabulary words by grouping them by parts of speech or other attributes;
- remembering foreign language vocabulary by grouping words into categories;
- organising historical information into time periods/events;
- if there is not a pattern in information, grouping items into threes or fours will still help your memory to retain them.

Chapter 6

Naming and rehearsal

This chapter looks at naming/rehearsal providing:

- an explanation of the strategy;
- an optional script for delivering the session;
- games for practising naming and rehearsal.

This technique involves the repetition of words, either silently to yourself (rehearsal) or quietly out loud (naming) so that they are more easily remembered. This is useful for remembering telephone numbers, lists of objects you need to collect or a sequence of tasks you need to do etc.

Optional script

If you want to remember a list of objects or numbers it can help if you repeat what you want to remember either inside your head or whisper the words quietly to yourself. Show children a small whiteboard and write this sequence of six numbers on it – 395781.

> I want to remember this number – but that is not easy and so to help myself I am going to say the number quietly to myself. I want you to check whether I have remembered it correctly.

Use the following method:

1 Place the whiteboard in a position where you cannot see the numbers but the children can while you are demonstrating quietly whispering the number repeatedly to yourself.
2 Call out the numbers that you can remember – it does not matter if you make mistakes – that will just demonstrate to the children that this is not easy even for grown-ups.
3 Rub the numbers out and replace them with a line of four new numbers. Ask the children to look at them and repeat them to themselves (either in their head or whispered to themselves). Turn the board so that they can no longer see the numbers and ask them what the numbers were.
4 To begin with encourage the group to work together to recall the numbers verbally, and gradually increase the number of digits to be remembered. Then increase the challenge of the game slightly by asking the children to write the numbers onto a whiteboard.

The challenge can be extended by increasing the amount of time the children are asked to remember the numbers for (putting the whiteboard on the other side of the room, or hiding the whiteboard so that the children have to look for it while remembering the number are fun ways to increase the challenge).

Memory club poster 2

Introduce the memory club poster. An A4 copy of the poster should be put up in the room where the group is being held to act as a memory aid. It will help with the transfer of skills between the group, the classroom and home if another copy is put on the classroom wall and children are given a smaller A5 copy to take home. Give children the parent information sheet on naming/rehearsal to take home at the end of the first session.

Games

Explain to the children that in all the games you are going to play you want them to try to remember by repeating what they want to remember either in their head or whispering it quietly to themselves.

Treasure hunt (with photocopiable page)

Before starting, use felt tips or coloured pencils to add colour to pictures so that objects that are present in more than one colour can be distinguished. Spread the treasure cards on a table and look through them together so that the children can name all the objects. Then put them on other side of the room so that the children will have to remember what they are going to collect while they walk to the picture cards. (These are in the photocopiable resources section.)

Explain to the children that they are going on a treasure hunt and will have to go to the other side of the room to collect their treasure. Tell them that they will be told exactly what they have to collect. The children take it in turns in pairs to be told which cards they need to go and collect. Encourage the children to repeat their list to each other as they look for the cards they need. This will encourage them to use the technique of repetition.

Start with the children collecting three cards and gradually ask them to collect one more each time, as long as they have achieved success on their previous attempt. To increase the challenge you can ask the children to work individually and either put the picture cards further away or spread them around the room so that they have to hunt for the picture and so remember for longer.

Table 6.1 List of treasure hunt loot

Gold watch	Gold cup	Gold jug
Gold crown	Blue ring	Red necklace
Jewelled bottle	Gold coin	Blue necklace
Red bottle	Green gem	Candlestick
Jewelled crown	Red gem	Gold bars
Diamond ring	Red ring	Money bags
Gold sword	Striped bottle	Medal
Treasure chest	Earrings	Gold trophy
Silver coins	Silver watch	Silver cup
Silver candlestick	Golden mirror	Neptune's trident

The following list of loot will help you to know what to ask them to collect:

Teaching point: counting items

Checking items off on our fingers is helpful as a indicator of how many items we need to remember and it can help trigger recall. If you have to remember four things, but can only remember three, knowing you need one more and going over the task of checking it off on our fingers can act as a trigger to either recall the item or ask for help to remember it.

Countdown

Play 'Kim's game' to demonstrate the usefulness of counting how many items you are trying to remember. Put 10 objects on a tray (do not tell the children how many there are) and explain to the children that they are going to try to remember all the things on the tray. Remind them to use rehearsal to help them to remember the objects. Give the children 30 seconds to look at the tray and then cover it and ask them to recall the objects. How do we know if we have got them all?

Explain to the children that it helps us to remember if we know how many things we need to recall. A useful way to do this is to count the items off on our fingers. Play Kim's Game again with 10 different objects to demonstrate this.

The rest of the games for practising naming/rehearsal can be played in any order. Choose ones that you think will appeal to the group you are working with – you do not have to play them all; once the children have mastered the strategy of rehearsal move on to the next strategy.

Spot the missing word

Tell the children that you are going to say some groups of words. Explain that after you say each group of words once, you will repeat them, but the second time you will leave one word out of the group. Ask them to tell you which word is missing.

Table 6.2 Example sentences for missing word game

Initial sentence	Sentence with missing word
Mouse, dog, cat	Mouse, cat
Pencil, chalk, crayon	Chalk, crayon
Nose, ears, eyes	Ears, eyes
Shark, whale, fish	Shark, fish
Apple, orange, banana, lemon	Apple, orange, lemon
Table, bed, television, bath	Table, television, bath
Trousers, socks, jumper, vest, hat	Trousers, socks, vest, hat

Make sure that you vary the position in the list of the missing word. Give the children time to make their own set of three words up and give them to the rest of the group, then once they are coping well with three words move on to four, then five up to a maximum of six. This game can also be played by the children in pairs.

Telephone numbers

The adult reads out the list of telephone numbers and the children repeat each set of numbers. When the children have grasped the game increase the difficulty by:

1   asking the children to enter the numbers on a calculator;
2   asking the children to write the numbers on a whiteboard.

With both of these variations the children must not start entering or writing the digits until the whole telephone number has been given and the numbers are shown to each other and compared and checked after each digit.

The difficulty can also be increased by lengthening the sequence of digits or increasing the delay between hearing the numbers and the children saying them. Once the children cope well with the number of digits in the telephone number, move to the next level.

Table 6.3 Telephone number game

Level 1 – three digits	Level 2 – four digits	Level 3 – five digits	Level 4 – six digits
179	3250	20845	639868
419	4962	29631	496179
864, etc.	9271, etc.	65972, etc.	324274, etc.

Colouring grids (with photocopiable page)

Each child has a copy of the colouring grid. Start with level 1 (three pieces of information) and move through the levels as the children are ready. Read out the list of colours, pausing between each set for the children to colour their grid. The children should not start colouring or selecting the pencils until the whole list has been read out. A way to help with this is to have the colours in a central pot and ask the children to turn their colouring face down, while they listen to the next list of colours to remember. The colouring pencils should be used in the order that they occur. Explain to the children that a colour may occur twice within the same grid. Example instructions:

Table 6.4 Example instructions for the colouring grid

Level 1 Three pieces of information	Level 2 Four pieces of information
Red, green, yellow	Yellow, red, green, green
Black, blue, red	Red, green, red, red
Orange, blue, red	Black, blue, orange, brown
Orange, grey, black	Green, pink, blue, green
Yellow, pink, blue	Blue, red, pink, orange

Level 3 Five pieces of information	Level 4 Six pieces of information
Black, green, red, brown, pink	Green, orange, brown, black, green, yellow
Green, red, orange green, yellow, red	Purple, brown, pink, blue, black, red
Red, pink, green, orange, yellow	Pink, blue, green, red, pink, orange
Orange, black, yellow, red, orange	Orange, grey, red, blue, yellow, blue
Yellow, red, red, pink, blue	Yellow, black, yellow, red, orange
Brown, yellow, blue, blue, black	Black, pink, blue, green, pink, blue
Blue, red, purple, orange, green	Red, pink, green, green, red, black

Remember this (game 1) (with photocopiable page)

Each child needs their own copy of the game picture grid from the photcopiable resources. Explain to the children that you are going to ask them to point to the pictures on the grid. Ask them to follow the directions only after you say the word 'NOW' – you can ask the children to turn their sheets face down between each turn and only turn them over when you say 'now' to ensure this.

Instructions

End each instruction by asking the children to turn over and point to the items now.

1 First point to the dog, then the pencils, then the ladybird.
2 Point to the triangle, the heart, the penguin and the elephant. What picture is above the last one you pointed to?

3 Point to the triangle, the gorilla, the wheel and the snail. What picture is below the last one you pointed to?

4 Find the flowers. Count three pictures left and one up. What is it?

5 Find the cheese. Count three down and two left. What is it?

6 Find the chick. Count down two pictures. What two pictures are either side of this one?

7 Find the apple. Count down three pictures. What two pictures are either side of this one?

8 Find the picture that is one picture up from the snowman and two pictures to the left.

9 Find the picture that is the last one in the second row and then up one picture.

10 Find the picture that is the second picture in the first row, then two down.

11 Find the picture that is the first picture in the third row and then two pictures down.

12 Find the pig and then count two pictures up and one picture to the left.

13 Find the picture that is next to the sheep, count four pictures up. What is it?

14 Find the picture that is above the kite, count three pictures right. What is it?

15 Find the picture that is between the star and the triangle. Count down three pictures. What is it?

Encourage the children to take it in turns to make up their own instructions.

Remember this! (game 2) (with photocopiable page)

Using the same grid, explain to the children that you are going to describe the pictures in the grid. Tell them that they must listen very carefully because sometimes you will be telling the truth but sometimes you will not. Tell them to put the grid face down each time you describe a picture. Then tell them to turn the sheets over and vote for either true or false. Gradually make the game more difficult by linking two and then three pieces of information.

Example sentences

1 The dog has a collar.
2 There are twelve flowers.
3 The ice cream has three scoops.
4 There are five candles on the birthday cake.
5 The snowman's hat is on his head.
6 The dog is in between the cloud and the pig.
7 There are seven animal pictures on the grid.
8 The ladybird has six spots and there are four bananas.
9 There are 11 different colours in the paint box.
10 There are six things to eat.
11 There are four things that can fly.

Encourage the children to take it in turns to make up their own true/false sentences.

Delete the number (with photocopiable page)

The adult acts as the caller and reads out the appropriate level of digits from the caller sheet. The children have their recording sheet on the table face down while the numbers are called out as they are not to start marking off the numbers until the whole list of numbers has been called. The children have to listen to the numbers and then mark them off on the bingo card in the same order as they are read out. After each string of numbers ask the children to compare the numbers they have deleted – has their neighbour deleted the same ones?

Table 6.5 Caller's sheet

Three digits	Four digits	Five digits	Six digits
6 2 7	2 5 3 7	4 9 0 3 2	3 4 8 1 9 2
3 9 5	5 8 3 2	2 4 7 1 3	2 4 1 7 8 3
1 9 4	5 7 0 2	5 8 6 8 4	7 1 0 3 6 4
8 3 4	4 7 0 2	1 5 3 7 6	6 8 7 5 1 2
9 3 6	1 4 7 5	3 4 8 6 7	8 5 3 2 7 1
	3 6 8 2	2 1 7 9 3	9 1 7 4 3 8
	3 7 5 2	1 5 3 9 6	6 9 1 4 3 5
	7 4 5 8	6 1 2 5 4	7 3 0 5 1 2
	8 1 6 4	1 8 6 0 5	2 1 6 4 7 0
	8 2 5 6	8 5 3 9 1	0 3 9 5 4 2
	4 6 2 8	8 4 4 3 6	7 8 1 3 4 2
	0 7 3 5	0 1 8 2 0	0 6 9 4 5 7
	6 2 3 1	8 4 5 1 6	5 1 0 8 3 4
	6 9 2 1	2 6 1 0 8	3 8 0 4 6 7
	3 5 1 7	3 8 1 7 1	7 3 9 1 6 5

Crazy cooks (with photocopiable pages)

Spread the ingredient cards on a table and look through them together so that the children can name all the ingredients. Then put them on the other side of the room or on a table outside in the corridor so that the children will have to remember their list while they walk to the table. Explain to the children that they are going to have to collect the correct ingredient cards to go with the recipe card that is read aloud to them. The children take it in turns in pairs to be told which cards they need to go and collect. Encourage the children to repeat their list to each other as they look for the card they need. This will encourage them to use the technique of repetition. Start with the children collecting three cards and gradually ask them to collect one more each time, as long as they have achieved success with their previous attempt.

Table 6.6 Ingredient cards

Chocolate	1 apple	2 strawberries
1 banana	butter	Grapes
3 bananas	cheese	1 orange
2 fish	milk	Pineapple
1 fish	cherries	Tomato
1 onion	flour	1 mushroom
1 carrot	1 egg	Honey
2 carrots	3 mushrooms	1 egg
2 apples	1 strawberry	4 tomatoes
Rice	Sugar	2 strawberries
Potatoes	2 sausages	

Moving day (with photocopiable page)

Each child and the adult organising the group will need their own copy of the house floor plans and the furniture cards (available in the photocopiable resources) in front of them. Start with simple instructions for putting two pieces of furniture into the different rooms of the house and then move on adding more pieces of furniture as the children are ready. Give the instructions to the children; they must listen to the full instruction before selecting the pieces of furniture and putting them in the correct rooms. Once the instructions are complete compare houses. Are they the same?

Phone factory (with photocopiable page)

The person giving the instructions is the boss and the listeners are the workers who colour the mobile phones. Start with the adult being the 'boss', but when the children are used to the game they can take it in turns to be the 'boss'. The children have to listen to the complete instructions before beginning to colour the mobile phone. When all the children have coloured their mobiles, compare them. If the children are sitting so that they cannot see how the others are colouring their phones they will have to rely on their memory.

Start with simple instructions giving the children two things to remember. If they cope well with this add extra tasks to remember, increasing by one extra task each time. For example, colour the screen red and all the buttons yellow. Here are some examples of different levels of instructions:

- Three pieces of information: colour the number buttons orange, the hash button green and the star button yellow.
- Four pieces of information: colour the screen blue, the top row of buttons yellow, the middle row green and the bottom row orange.
- Five pieces of information: colour the antenna black, the screen yellow, the body of the phone green, the number buttons blue and the other buttons orange.

Online resources

Memory IV game

The children have to memorise the sequence of objects shown and then repeat the sequence by clicking on the objects. The game starts with a short sequence which is extended as the children successfully reproduce the sequence. Available at:

http://thekidzpage.com/freekidsgames/games/ngames/memory4/memory4-game.html

Celebrity Simon

There are nine different famous people, each of whom makes a different funny noise. The game gives a sequence of celebrities/noises and the child has to repeat this in the same sequence by clicking on the picture of the celebrity. Just as in the traditional Simon game the sequence of noises to repeat gets longer and longer until the player makes a mistake. Available at:

http://thekidzpage.com/freekidsgames/games/celebrity_simon/simon-online-game.html

Trolley dash

In this game the children are given a shopping list (with pictures as well as words), they then have to go along the supermarket conveyor belt and click on all the items in their shopping list before the shopping time runs out. The time limit makes this quite challenging, so this game is best for children who have good mouse control. Available at:

http://gamesgames.com/game/Trolley_Dash.html

Chapter 7

Visualisation

This chapter looks at visualisation, providing:

* an explanation of the strategy;
* an optional script for delivering the session;
* games for practising visualisation.

Visualisation is using the technique of making mental images to aid memory. It involves making a mental picture in your head so that you can remember. When we make an internal visual image of information we have heard, it helps us to remember the information. It can be useful for remembering the main points in a text.

Optional script

Today we are going to try a new way of helping to remember things. Close your eyes and listen carefully as I tell you about my house. As I am telling you, try to make a picture in your head of what my house looks like. My house has white walls and a red roof. It has a green front door and four square windows. On the left of my house is a large apple tree and there is a swing hanging from the tree. To the right of my house is my garage, the garage door is green like the front door. There is a gold number 10 on the front door and a chimney on the roof.

Open your eyes – now can you use your picture to answer my questions? Try closing your eyes and looking at your picture if you can't remember.

What colour is the front door?

What number is my house?

How many windows does it have?

What is in my garden?

Activities to practise visualisation

Enhancing visual memory

Take an object or picture, ask the children to study it for 20 seconds, cover the object and try to recall as many details of the object as possible. The object/picture that you choose should have plenty of detail for the children to study.

When you have remembered everything you can, look again and take in more details. Close your eyes and add your new observations to your original mental picture. Then open your eyes again, take in more detail, close your eyes and review your mental picture. Repeat until you cannot find any new features. Remove the object from sight.

Ask the group to answer questions about the object – encourage them to use the mental picture they have created to help them.

Practising description

Ask the children to think about what a particular object looks like (e.g. a cat they know). Stress to the children that each of their mental pictures will be different as they are thinking about different cats. Ask each child to describe the colour of the thing they can see in their head. Ask for further details, for example, size, shape, special features, etc. Demonstrate this activity as a group and then pair the children up to practise. After pair work ask them to feed back about the details from their partner's picture. List of possible objects:

- Dog/cat/fish, etc. or other pets
- Favourite toy
- Family car
- School bag
- A fire engine
- A police car
- Your favourite place.

Using your imagination to the full

Encouraging the children to add all their senses into the pictures they create in their heads can make this task more multi-sensory and help them to remember.

Optional script

> We often need to remember to do things that are not that interesting and so are not easy to remember, e.g. remembering to give a note to your mum after school. However, if we use our imagination to make the picture in our head of what we need to do more interesting, then we can make it more exciting and easier to remember. If we add imaginary smells, sensations and noises we make the image even more memorable.
>
> For example, imagine that you need to remember to post an important letter. First, picture the ordinary envelope, then change this picture to make it more interesting and easier to remember. For example, picture yourself staggering along the road with an enormous golden envelope. The envelope is decorated with sparkling, flashing red lights. It smells of chocolate and is making a buzzing noise. The envelope feels cold to touch and your fingers are freezing.

Each child has a letter in an envelope that they are going to be asked to give to their parents tonight. Give each child time to develop their own personal memory story to help them to remember to deliver the letter. Remind them to include imaginary smells, sensations and noises. Allow the children time to share their memory stories with the group. At the end of the session, send the children to put the letters into their school bags so that they will have to remember them at the end of the day. (The envelope contains the letter to parents that accompanies information sheet 2, on visualisation. See the Resources chapter.)

Memory club poster 3

The key is to see; make a picture in your head and remember what's been said. An A4 copy of the poster is put up in the room where the group is being held to act as a memory aid. It will help with the transfer of skills between the group, the classroom and home if another copy is put on the classroom wall and children are given a smaller A5 copy to take home.

Games

Driving through a picture

Give each child a copy a photocopy of the same scene. Any picture with lots of detail will be suitable for this game. Explain that we will travel through the scene, looking carefully at all the objects on the way. Help the children to link the objects together to create a story/visual in their minds. After a few minutes of creating the mental picture, remove the scene from the children and see if they can recall the scene naming aloud specific objects, preferably in order.

Storytelling

Explain that you are going to tell a story and the children are going to try to visualise the important parts of the story in their minds. Ask them to close their eyes and make pictures in their heads for the story as they listen.

> Once upon a time a small boy called Sam was playing with his ball in the garden. He gave the ball a big kick and it went down the old well. Sam lent over the wall of the well to see if he could see his ball, but he lent too far, over balanced and fell down the well. He landed at the bottom with a splash. Luckily he did not hurt himself, but the sides of the well were steep and smooth and it was impossible for Sam to climb out. It was dark in the bottom of the well and there was water, but luckily it only came up to Sam's knees. The water was cold and smelly. Sam shouted for help, but no one heard him. He was cold and scared. As Sam's eyes got used to the dark he started to feel his way around the walls of the well. The walls were smooth and for a long time he did not find anything that would help him, but he kept going, partly to try to keep warm. He had been going round and round the well for ages when his fingers felt a little bump in the smooth cold wall. Sam's cold fingers explored the round shape. It felt like a piece of brick that was sticking out of the wall. He tried to push on the circle, but nothing happened. He tried twisting it – still nothing. It was when he pulled the mysterious round shape that things started to happen . . .

Ask the children questions about the story, encouraging them to close their eyes and recreate their mental picture to help them to find the answer.

This activity can be extended by asking the children to work in pairs to create an end to the story. They can then tell their ending to the rest of group while they close their eyes and make a mental picture of the ending.

Repeat the game, selecting a short story that is unfamiliar to the children. At the end of the story ask the children some questions relating directly to the text. You can increase the difficulty of the questions as the children are able. Finally, ask the children to describe some of their internal images. If the book has pictures you can then compare these mental images with those in the book.

Making memory movies

In this activity the children are going to make their own inner movie to help them to remember a sequence. Explain to the children that making their movie as colourful, exciting and exaggerated as possible will help them to remember. Making the film funny is also a very useful memory aid. Using their imagination to the full will make what they are trying to remember more interesting and so more memorable. Involving all your senses, including sounds, smells, tastes and sensations as well as sights, will also make the movie more memorable.

Practise this technique together to remember the sequence of this simple recipe. Remind the children that when you cook it is important to remember things in the right order or your finished cakes may not turn out right.

Recipe to remember: mix together butter and sugar, add an egg and some vanilla essence. Add the flour and mix well. Put in the cake cases and bake for 20 minutes.

Encourage the children to help you make up a memory movie for this, adding in their ideas to make the movie more interesting. For example, they have to get the butter out of a cow, the sugar comes in lumps and they have to jump on it first to break the lumps, chase a chicken for the egg, etc.

When the whole recipe has been put into the memory movie ask the children to sit and replay the movie in their head. Now, together, can you remember the recipe in the correct sequence?

This technique is also useful for remembering the sequence of instructions for science experiments or the plot of a story. Before moving on try to repeat this strategy with something from the children's current class topic as this will help them link the intervention work back to the classroom.

Chapter 8

Visualisation and repetition

This chapter looks at combining two strategies, visualisation and repetition, providing:

- an explanation of the strategy;
- an optional script for delivering the session;
- games for practising using visual organisation strategies.

Explain to the children that they can use more than one strategy at a time to help them to remember and that there are times when using two strategies together will help them to remember more.

Optional script

Today we are going to use both of our memory strategies at the same time, so we are going to make pictures in our heads and also repeat the names of the objects in the pictures quietly to ourselves.

Games

Magic potions (with photocopiable page)

Before starting, use felt tips or coloured pencils to add colour to pictures so that objects that are present in more than one colour can be distinguished. You are going to make up a magic potion. It is important with a magic potion that you get your recipe exactly the same every time. Show the children the picture cards with the choice of ingredients. Demonstrate choosing three cards and then making mental pictures of the objects while also quietly repeating the objects' names.

The children choose their cards, starting with three ingredients. Encourage them to make a visual picture of their ingredients and also repeat the objects to themselves. Turn over the cards. Can they remember their ingredients?

Repeat the process, adding an extra ingredient each time until you reach the limits of the children's memory. The challenge level of this game can also be extended by increasing the delay between memorising and recalling the objects, or by having a second set of pictures on the other side of the room and asking the children to go and find the ingredients from among them.

Online resources

Memory test

In this game the children are presented with a brick wall, during the game the bricks in the wall gradually become different colours. The challenge for the children is to remember where the different colour bricks are and the order in which they appear so that they can colour in their own wall in exactly the same way after the target wall has disappeared. The game starts with just a couple of target bricks and gradually adds more and more as the children succeed. Available at:

http://gamesgames.com/game/memory-test.html

Chapter 9

Keywords for meaning

This chapter looks at identifying keywords, providing:

- an explanation of the strategy;
- an optional script for delivering the session;
- games for practising identifying keywords and images.

Keywords are the main ideas in a message. When we talk, we add a lot of extra words around the key ideas. For example, 'Look at the time, it's getting late, if we don't hurry we are going to be late for school. Hurry up and go and clean your teeth and brush your hair. Make sure you have put your reading book in your school bag and don't forget your lunchbox.' Below, the keywords are in italics.

> Look at the time, it's getting late, if we don't *hurry* we are going to be late for school. Hurry up and go and clean your *teeth* and brush your *hair*. Make sure you have put your *reading book* in your school bag and don't forget your *lunchbox*.

This links back to both rehearsal and visualisation, because it is really only the keywords that need to be rehearsed or visualised. It is only essential that this important information is remembered – anything else is a bonus! For older children using the programme, being able to highlight the keywords they are hearing is a useful precursor to note taking.

Optional script

> When we talk we include a lot of extra information and trying to remember everything is not necessary. Listen to this sentence and try to spot the keywords to remember. Look for the words with the most important information.
>   It's time to put on your pyjamas, clean your teeth and go to bed.
>   The key words are; it's time to put on your *pyjamas*, clean your *teeth* and go to *bed*.

Games

Ask the children to identify the keyword(s) in the sentence, and then ask them to recall the sentence. You can increase the challenge of the task by adding in extra adjectives that the children need to discard.

Listening for keywords

- When I am making a cake I use flour.
- When I am making a cake I use flour and sugar.
- When I am making a cake I like to use flour, sugar and butter.
- When I am making a cake I like to use flour, sugar and butter and it is important to use eggs.
- When I am making a cake I use always flour, sugar and eggs and I like to use butter and vanilla.
- I hurt my leg.
- I fell off my bike and I hurt my leg and back.
- I fell off my bike and hurt my leg, my back and I cut my finger.
- I fell off my bike on the way to school and I hurt my leg and my back and I cut my finger and knee.
- I fell off my bike on the way to school and I hurt my leg and my back and I cut my finger and knee. As I fell off I bumped my head on the pavement.
- At the zoo I saw a lion.
- Yesterday when I was at the zoo I saw a lion and a giraffe.
- Yesterday when I was at the zoo I saw a lion and there was a big enclosure with a giraffe and a zebra.
- Yesterday when I was at the zoo I saw a lion and there was a big enclosure with a giraffe and a zebra. Next to the giraffe and the zebra were the elephants.
- Yesterday when I was at the zoo I saw a lion and there was a big enclosure with a giraffe and a zebra. Next to the giraffe and the zebra were the elephants, but my favourites were the monkeys.
- At the beach I ate some candy floss.
- At the beach I ate candy floss and then I had a lemonade ice lolly.
- At the beach I ate candy floss and then I had a lemonade ice lolly for my elevenses and I had some chips for my lunch.
- At the beach I ate candy floss and then I had a lemonade ice lolly for my elevenses and I had some chips for my lunch. I had a hot dog with ketchup with my chips.
- At the beach I ate candy floss and then I had a lemonade ice lolly for my elevenses and I had some chips for my lunch. I had a hot dog with ketchup with my chips. In the afternoon I had a big chocolate ice cream.

Memory club poster 4

Give the children the information sheet for parents about keywords (3 Keywords for meaning, p. 83). An A4 copy of the poster is put up in the room where the group is being held to act as a memory aid. It will help with the transfer of skills between the group, the classroom and home if another copy is put on the classroom wall and children are given a smaller A5 copy to take home.

Chapter 10

Keywords and visualisation

This chapter looks at combining two strategies, keywords and visualisation, providing:

- an explanation of the strategy;
- an optional script for delivering the session;
- games for practising using visual organisation strategies.

Just as focusing on the keywords can help you to remember verbal information, focusing on the key features of a picture will help to remember visual information. By combining the skill of finding the keywords/features of objects to put into your mental picture and visualisation to help build up a mental picture of the objects you need to remember, you can increase the amount you can remember.

Optional script

Today we are going to use our skill of looking for the keywords in the information we are trying to remember at the same time as making pictures in our heads. Using more than one memory skill at a time can really help increase the amount you can remember. As you listen to the story I am going to tell you and find keywords use those words to make your visual picture.

Games

Remember the treasure (with photocopiable pages)

Tell the children they are going to listen to your story and try to build up a picture in their heads. Remind them to look for the keywords in the story so that they will know what to put into their picture.

Script 1

I found this box in a charity shop. It is made of wood and has circles carved into the wood of the lid. In the middle of each circle there is a jewel. In the middle of the lid the jewels in the circles are red and around the edge they are green. In the very centre of the lid there is one large blue jewel that sparkles in the light. The sides of the box are also carved with circles but there are no jewels in these. Around the bottom of the sides there is a wide gold line that runs all around the box. In the middle of the front side there is a large letter A carved in the wood and painted with gold.

Discuss the keywords: box, charity shop, wood, carved circles, jewels – red and green, large blue jewel, gold stripe, gold 'A' on front. Ask the children to answer the following true or false questions.

1   The box is made from glass.
2   The box has the letter E on it.
3   I found the box in the toy shop.
4   The letter A is on the lid.
5   The large jewel on the top is green.

Give the children the resources sheet for this activity and ask them to colour the lid and front of the box as accurately as they can from their mental picture.

Script 2

I found this bottle when I was diving in the Red Sea. I was deep down at the bottom of the sea, past the coral and colourful fish. On the rocky bottom of the sea I found a cave and inside the cave it was very, very dark, but in the light of my torch I saw something blue and gold shine. It was an old bottle. The bottle was made of blue glass and had a golden stopper in the top. The bottle was next to a big shell and a strange looking crab-like creature. I carefully picked it up. All over the blue bottle there were small golden stars that made the bottle feel bumpy and on the top of the stopper there was a large red jewel.

Discuss the keywords: Red Sea, cave, blue glass, golden stopper, small golden stars, red jewel. Ask the children to answer the following true or false questions.

1   I found this at the bottom of the blue sea.
2   It is made of blue glass.
3   It has big silver stars on it.
4   The stopper is golden.
5   The jewel on the stopper is green.

Deep sea diver (with photocopiable pages)

Before starting, use felt tips or coloured pencils to add colour to pictures so that objects that are present in more than one colour can be distinguished. In this game the children are going to be divers collecting treasure from under the sea. Remind the children of the techniques of visualisation and identifying the keywords. Explain that they are going to need to use the techniques of identifying the keywords to see what they need to collect and try to use visualisation to help them remember what it is.

Set the scene by describing the underwater cave that we are going to enter. The cave contains lots of amazing treasures, however, we must only collect the treasure that we have been told to collect or the mouth of the cave will close, trapping us inside. Spread the treasure cards on a table and look through them together so that they children can name all the objects. Some children like to recreate the cave by putting the cards under a table to 'dive' under during the game! Do the first turn together to demonstrate to the children how the game works.

Script 1

Dive deep to the bottom of the sea and find the opening to the underwater treasure cave. While you are inside you must only touch the treasure you have been asked to collect. You may pick up a beautiful golden crown, the large sparkling ruby and the golden candlestick. Do not touch anything else.

Work together to isolate the keywords, and then give the children time to generate their own mental image of the objects. How many objects are we looking for? Remind the children that knowing how many is a useful way to check you have it right. Together look through the treasure cards to locate the correct one.

On the children's turns, introducing a little distance between where the group is sitting and the location of the 'cave' will add more challenge to the game.

For each turn repeat Script 1 inserting different objects from the treasure list. The challenge can be increased by adding extra non-essential adjectives like sparkling, amazing, beautiful, etc. When the children are skilled at this the difficulty of the game can be increased by including treasure items that they must not touch into the script; this will make isolating the keywords more difficult and will introduce interference to their visualisation, making it more difficult to locate the correct treasure card.

Script 2

Dive deep to the bottom of the sea and find the opening to the underwater treasure cave. While you are inside you must only touch the treasure that you have been asked to collect. You may pick up a golden crown, but do not touch the big, heavy treasure chest. You may pick up the beautiful large ruby but not the gorgeous diamond. Bring the golden candlestick, but do not touch the golden sword. Do not touch anything else.

Gold watch	Gold cup	Gold jug
Gold crown	Blue ring	Red necklace
Jewelled bottle	Gold coin	Blue necklace
Red bottle	Green gem	Candle stick
Jewelled crown	Red gem	Gold bars
Diamond ring	Red ring	Money bags
Gold sword	Striped bottle	Medal
Treasure chest	Earrings	Gold trophy
Silver coins	Silver watch	Silver cup
Silver candlestick	Golden mirror	Neptune's trident

Figure 10.1 Object list

Story time

Remind the children of the story time activity they used to practise visualisation. This time they are also going to use the technique of identifying the keywords to help decide the key items to put into their picture.

Script

One day a group of children decided to go for a picnic in the woods. They all packed up some delicious things to eat. They had lots of sandwiches, but also lots of crisps, cake and chocolate biscuits. They decided to go to the woods on their bikes and they cycled quickly to the woods and left their bikes under the big oak tree on the edge of the wood. They had a fantastic time in the woods playing games, climbing trees and eating lots of food, until one of them noticed that it was starting to get dark. The children were a bit worried about being so late home so they quickly gathered up all the picnic things and set off to find their bikes. Unfortunately as the wood started to get dark, everything started to look different and the children walked for what felt like ages looking for their bikes.

Discuss with the children what objects they put in their picture – what are the key objects in the story sequence? If the children are finding this challenging, reread the story giving them each a whiteboard to draw their pictures on as you read. Remind them that they only need the keywords.

Repeat this process with another short story unfamiliar to the children. At the end of the story ask the children some questions relating directly to the text. You can increase the difficulty of the questions as the children become more skilled at this strategy. Finally, ask the children to describe some of their internal images. If the book has pictures you can then compare these mental images with those in the book if you are using a picture book.

There are a number of free online games that make this activity more appealing to the children.

Online resources

Mental training – visual challenge – odd one out

In this game you simply have to click on the person who is different from the other three. The game starts simply by asking the children to spot very obvious differences, but as they succeed the differences become far more difficult to spot and they will need to look very closely to find them.

http://gamesgames.com/game/Mental-Training---Visual-Challenge.html

Mental training – visual challenge – odd one out – geometric shapes (dis-symmetry)

In this game you simply have to click on the shape that is different from the other three. The game starts simply by asking the children to spot very obvious differences, but as they succeed the differences become far more difficult to spot and they will need to look very closely to find them. The game also makes it more difficult to spot the differences by putting their shape in different orientations. This game is more difficult than the person game (above) on the same website.

http://gamesgames.com/game/Mental-Training---Visual-Challenge.html

I lost my puppy

This game involves studying a 'photograph' of a missing dog and then identifying that dog from the dogs in the park. The game starts simply by asking the children to distinguish between two very different dogs in the park, however, it becomes more difficult as they succeed as the dogs are made more similar and more dogs are introduced.

http://gamesgames.com/game/i-lost-my-puppy.html

Find the suspect

This game presents you with a number of faces to memorise. Starting with just one and increasing in number if you are successful. These target faces then disappear and you then have to identify the 'suspect' from the new faces you are shown. This game is made easier if you focus on the key distinctive features of each face.

http://thekidzpage.com/freekidsgames/games/nggames/suspect-game1.html

Chapter 11

Chaining and linking

This chapter looks at chaining/linking, providing:

- an explanation of the strategy;
- an optional script for delivering the session;
- games for practising chaining and linking.

Another strategy to support memory is association, or trying to connect each word/event or fact to a familiar person, place, thing, feeling or situation. Chaining or linking ideas helps children to remember information because it helps them to group items together. One way of linking is to use categories; another is to link items that need to be remembered from different categories together using a silly story or picture; yet another is to link the information to be remembered to something you already know, like a memory, character, song, rhyme or rhythm.

Optional script 1

Today we are going to look at a new way to help us remember. We are going to try to link together the things that we are trying to remember by making a chain to link up the information we want to remember. There are several ways we can try to link information together. First, we are going to link the names of the objects we want to remember together by putting objects into categories. The first category we are going to use is food.

The adult says their food, '*spaghetti*', and stands up to start a line (the chain). Each child is asked to stand up one at a time in the line and add a new food. When everyone is in the line, try to remember all the foods. Add to the challenge by going down the line twice so that everyone has two turns to add a word. The game can be repeated with other categories: sports, TV programmes, sweets, clothes, animals, toys, pets, drinks, places.

Memory club poster 5

Give the children the information sheet for parents about linking/chaining activities.

Games

I went shopping

Sit in a circle. The adult starts the game by saying, 'I went shopping and I bought an apple'. The next player continues, 'I went shopping and I bought an apple and a cake'. Every player adds a new item after recalling all the others. Encourage the children to link the object to the person who said it. If they cannot recall an item the people who added them to the list can offer them a clue.

My favourite things

Different people like different favourite foods. We are going to try to remember everyone's favourite foods. Explain that linking ideas helps us to remember things. Go round the circle starting with the group leader who says 'my name is . . . . and I like . . . .'

The next person starts by looking at the leader and repeating 'her name is . . . . and she likes . . . . ; my name is . . . . and I like . . . .'

Go round the circle adding names and favourite foods. Every person starts by listing the names and foods of all the rest of the group before adding their own. An adaptation of the game is to list everyone's favourite TV programmes, animals, sports, etc.

Once the group become skilled at this (or with smaller groups) you can go round the circle again, either adding a second favourite food each or an item from a second catagory, e.g. 'My name is Tom and I like spaghetti and playing tennis.'

The previous games are practising remembering information within one category. The next game encourages the children to sort information they have been given into categories.

Sort the stuff

Use a selection of picture cards that have been made for any of the other games. You need enough for every child to have about five cards each. At the beginning of the game each player may choose a category by looking at the pictures they have, for example, food, animals, etc. Deal the cards out and the children can take it in turns to go round the table and lay a card in one of the named categories. The aim is to get rid of your cards first.

Optional script 2

There is another way that you can use chaining/linking to help you to remember and that is using a silly story.

The words we are trying to remember are: elephant, swimming pool, golden crown, fish and chips, helicopter and mountain.

Listen carefully to this story: one day a large, grey elephant went for a dip at the swimming pool. He dived down to the bottom of the pool and found a golden crown. He picked it up and wore it home. On the way home he was very hungry after all his swimming so he had fish and chips for tea. Then he was tired so he could not walk any further and so he got a helicopter back to his mountain home.

Encourage the children to visualise the story quietly to themselves. Can they retell the story as a group? Ask the children if together they can recall all the six target objects.

Games

Story telling

Give the children a new set of target words to remember: star, house, doughnut, alien, racing car, fairy. Write a list or draw quick pictures on the whiteboard to act as cues while they are making the story. Start the story for the children:

One night there was a bright star, it was so bright that it woke up a little boy. He came out of his house . . .

• Encourage the children to complete the story with you. When the story is finished ask the children to retell it to each other from the beginning using the pictures. Also ask them, what are the six keywords that we are remembering?

- Rub out the words/pictures from the board and ask the children to retell the story to each other from the beginning, without using the pictures. Also ask them, what are the six keywords that we are remembering?
- Give the children this different set of words to make their own stories and repeat the whole process again (cup, coat, sun, hippopotamus, ice cream, mouse).
- Encourage the children to visualise the story quietly to themselves. Can they retell the story as a group? Ask the children if together they can recall all the six target objects.

Word sets for other stories

1   Rainbow, mountain, horse, boat, road, bed, chocolate cake.
2   Horse, nurse, car, shoe, sea, snowman, ball.
3   Road, milk, tractor, star, dog, doughnut.
4   Bus, tree, clock, puddle, snake, hat.
5   Sea, rain, shop, train, castle, cot.
6   Coat, hammer, ice, window, computer, man, wheel.
7   Baby, phone, button, igloo, flower, sheep.

Optional script 3

You can also try to remember objects by linking them with something you already know. When you have to learn something new, just connect the new information with a person, thing, event, movie, or any strong association to help you remember it. For example, remembering the date 12 May: by remembering that it is the month before my birthday (April) and the digits are reversed (12 instead of 21).

Look at some of the topic-specific information/vocabulary that the children are currently using in class and use the strategy of linking to a person/character to help to remember them.

Games

Song words

Some people find that putting a list of words to be remembered into a favourite song and singing them to themselves aids their memory. Try putting this list of equipment into a song: ruler, pencil, sharpener, book, P.E kit, homework, lunchbox, coat – these fit to the beginning of 'Twinkle, twinkle little star' – not the coolest song choice but it will be one all the children know and it will give them the idea!

Sing it together a few times, then send one of the children off round the room to see if they can collect the right equipment. Repeat the game using different objects and the children's choice of song. If the children manage this number of objects, extend the list of equipment to increase the challenge. Repeat the activity with music of the children's choice.

Rhyming

Many children use the alphabet song to help them to learn the alphabet – this uses the rhythm of a song and the support of rhyme to learn the alphabet. Another popularly used rhyme is 'i before e except after c'. Look together at the memory club posters – can the children remember any of the phrases from these? Highlight the rhyme in these.

Drumming

Some people find that linking words to be remembered to a rhythm aids their memory – a bit like a rap! They are linking the words to the rhythm.

Try clapping and chanting this list of equipment several times: lunch box, pencil, book, protractor. Then just clap the rhythm and don't say the words – everyone will automatically say them in their heads! Now send one of the children off round the room to see if they can collect the right equipment.

If the children manage this, extend the list of equipment. Do not try to remember more than three or four different lists using rhythm in one session, otherwise the children may begin to confuse them and then it will not help their memory. There are some great educational raps freely available on YouTube that exploit the power of rhythm and music to help boost memory and it is worth exploring some of these with your group.

Mnemonics

Optional script

> A useful way of trying to remember information is simply playing with the first letters of words to make a sentence to help you remember. This works by making the information you want to remember more memorable and is particularly useful for remembering information in a particular order. All you do is take the first letter of each word you want to learn and make another word.

Well-known mnemonics include:

- 'Richard of York gave battle in vain' for remembering the sequence of the colours of the rainbow – red, orange, yellow, green, blue, indigo, violet.
- 'Never eat shredded wheat' for remembering the points of the compass – north, south, east, and west.

My very easy method just speeds up names for naming planets in order – Mercury, Venus, Earth, Mars, Jupiter, Saturn, Uranus, Neptune. Can the children find any more?

Practise this skill by linking the activity to the current topics that the children are studying in class. Ask the class teachers for some suitable information from the topic that you can work with the children to develop a mnemonic for.

Chapter 12

Visualisation and linking

This chapter looks at combining two strategies, visualisation and linking, providing:

- an explanation of the strategy;
- an optional script for delivering the session;
- games for practising using visual organisation strategies.

Linking two strategies can add to the impact that they have on your memory. Encourage the children to start making a mental picture of the associations they are making to support their memory.

Activity

The journey

This system links together the skills of visualisation and association and is useful for remembering a list of information. Start by using a familiar journey – I imagine that I am walking from Class 3 in my school to the to the staff room. I come out of the classroom door, along the landing, down the stairs, turn the corner and go through the double doors, along the corridor past the doors to classes 2 and 1 and through the double doors. I go through the cloakroom, and along the corridor by the bell rope, past the old front door and through the ICT suite and turn right into the staffroom.

We are going to use a journey like this to help us to remember a list of 13 objects by imagining that we are walking through the school and we see the objects on our list at certain points along the way. Here is an example of a script for my journey; you will of course have to write your own, to make this relevant to a location that your children know.

Example script

Close your eyes and imagine you are walking through the school, imagine the objects on the way.

You come out of the classroom door, Michael Jackson is standing by the door. On the landing there is a big bunch of red flowers. Halfway down the stairs there is a chocolate cake and at the bottom of the stairs is a toilet; turn the corner and go through the double doors – Mickey Mouse holds the doors open for you. Go along the corridor past the door to Class 2. In the doorway there is a tub of ice cream. Carry on along the corridor, outside Class 1 there is a basket of fruit. On the blue double doors there is a monkey. Go through the double door and into the cloakroom. In the cloakroom there is large TV. Go through the cloakroom, and along the corridor by the bell rope; under the bell rope there is a plate of cheese sandwiches. Go past the old front door. On the floor by the door is a bucket of milk, and continue through the ICT suite. On one of the tables there is a packet of chocolate biscuits. Go into the staff room. On the sofa you see David Beckham.

Ask the children to repeat this journey in their head again seeing all the objects as they walk. Now as a group talk through the journey and see if you can remember all 13 objects in order. If some of the group are finding this a challenge, repeat the process of reading the script with the children visualising and then try to recall the list again.

This activity is best done near the beginning of the session so that it is possible to run another activity and then return to this at the end of the session to see if the children can still remember their list. If they are successful in this, extend the challenge by sending the letter to parents that accompanies this activity home. This asks the parents to ask their child to try to recall the list at home that evening.

This activity should only be done once in a session – to repeat it more than this will confuse the children as to which set of images the objects to be remembered belong to. It would be best to run this activity with a different object list over several different sessions.

Chapter 13

Visual organisers for information

This chapter looks at using visual organisation strategies, providing:

- an explanation of the strategy;
- an optional script for delivering the session;
- games for practising using visual organisation strategies.

Organising information and sorting it onto a diagram can be a very useful memory tool. The act of sorting makes the pupils engage with the material and also helps to ensure comprehension, which in itself will support memory. In addition to this, organising information in a visual way can be a powerful memory tool. These tools help pupils to see the things they are trying to learn and help them to organise information. There are many different types of visual organisation strategies.

Mind maps

Mind maps work well because they use several memory tools, including visual images, imagination and association. Mind maps use words, phrases and pictures to record ideas and include lines to organise these ideas into areas and to show the connections between these different areas. Lots of examples of mind maps are freely available on the Internet – try typing 'mind map' into Google so that you can show the children examples.

Optional script

Today we are going to look at a way of making a map to help us to remember the information. We can use colours, pictures and words to help us to remember. I am going to make a small mind map of some of the things I know about cats, so I write cats in this box and the three things I know in the other boxes.

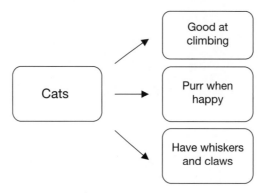

Figure 13.1 Example mind map

Steps in mind map drawing

1 Start by asking the children to link three pieces of information they know about a topic. Good choices of topics are animals, fruits, foods, transport, sports, pop stars, celebrities, TV programmes or characters, films, etc. Give the whole group the same topic, for example, animals. Encourage the group to share what they have done.
2 Move on to asking the children to record more pieces of information on a different topic. Some children respond to the idea of the octopus and needing to put a piece of information on each leg.
3 While others will find the visual image of the sun and putting a piece of information onto each ray more useful.

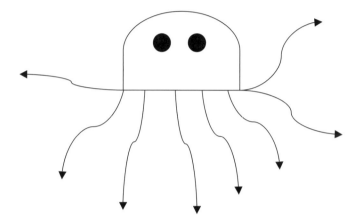

Figure 13.2 Example of an octopus map

Figure 13.3 Example of a sun map

Give the group the chance to experiment with each using some of the simple topics suggested and to share their work so that they can learn from each other. The next step is to develop the children's understanding that one piece of information may lead onto several more. The sun template can be useful here if the children are encouraged to put more arrow rays coming out from the main rays. For example, if completing a map for transport, one of the main rays could be train, which could then have new arrows for the information stands, ticket, station and diesel.

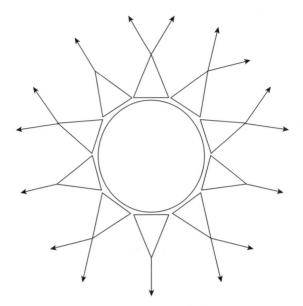

Figure 13.4 Example of a sun template

An alternative map shape that some children find useful is the tree; putting information at the different points on the branches can help to show how the information fits together.

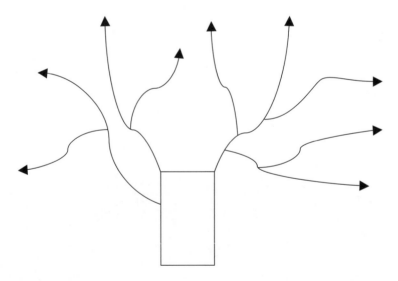

Figure 13.5 Example of a tree map

This series of steps will give the children the skills they need to draw a mind map.

Important things to remember when making mind maps

1   Start by drawing a circle in the middle of a piece of paper and writing the name of the topic for your mind map in the circle.
2   Add a picture to this circle to support your memory.

3 Use colours to boost your memory.
4 Draw some branches to divide the topic into main areas.
5 Draw curved branches to link the areas of information.
6 Add one keyword per branch.
7 Add images throughout.

Creating a memory strategy mind map

To encourage the children to put everything they have learned about mind mapping together you are going to work as a group to make a mind map for memory strategies. You need a large sheet of plain paper and coloured pens. Work together as a group to create a mind map for the memory techniques that you have covered so far. Start by drawing a picture in the middle that will help to trigger the children's memories (for example, a brain with eyes, arms and legs). Make full use of different colours, pictures and symbols on the map (everything does not need to be written in words). Encourage the children to use their imagination to make the different areas of the mind map more memorable. Keep this mind map on the wall as a memory aid during the rest of the course.

A website that will convert a list of keywords or text into a mind map for you is http://text2mindmap.com. This is useful to show examples to children who have never used this technique themselves, or if you want something 'beautiful' for a display. However, it is the processes involved in making up your own mind map – linking the ideas together and using different colours, words and images to record them – that actually form the memory links in your head and so help you to remember. Using this website is not a good idea if the aim of making the mind map is as a memory tool.

Memory club poster 6

Give the children the information sheet number 6 about visual organisation strategies to give to their parents.

Cause and effect diagrams (with photocopiable page)

The boxes for a mind map can be organised to show cause and effect by placing the event in the middle box, the causes in the left boxes and the effects listed in the right boxes. (The effects and the causes are connected to the event by lines.)

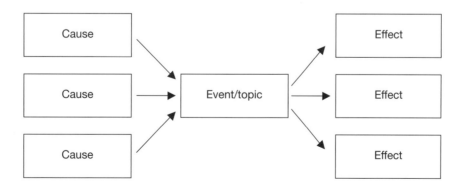

Figure 13.6 A cause and effect diagram

Cause and effect sorting cards (with photocopiable pages)

Give the children a copy of the cause and effect sorting diagram from the photocopiable resources and a set of sorting cards. Encourage them to work in pairs to sort the cards on to the diagram and then compare the different diagrams produced when they have finished. Topic cards included are autumn, summer, photosynthesis and 'Torch story'.

Sequence diagrams (with photocopiable page)

The boxes on mind maps can be organised to show the order of a sequence of events.

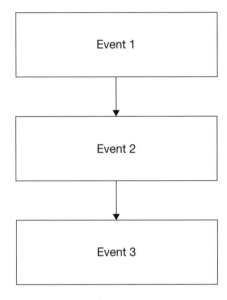

Figure 13.7 A sequence diagram

Story sequencing

Practise using the sequencing diagram by using one of the stories provided in the resources. Can the children organise the main events of a story onto the sequence diagram?

Venn diagrams (with photocopiable page)

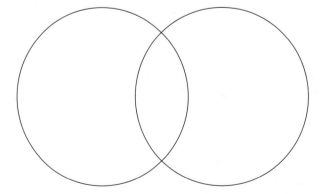

Figure 13.8 A venn diagram

Venn diagrams are very useful for comparing and contrasting two related areas of knowledge, with similarities between the two areas being in the middle section and differences in the outer areas.

Give the children a copy of the Venn diagram from the photocopiable resources and a set of sorting cards. Encourage them to work in pairs to sort the cards on to the diagram and then compare the different diagrams produced when they have finished.

Sort numbers from 0–40 into those that are multiples of 2 and multiples of 5.
Sort numbers from 0–40 into those that are multiples of 5 and even numbers.
Sort names of children in the group into those who like pizza and those who like salad.
Sort words into those with an e and those with a t.
Sort football teams by the colours of their strip. (photocopiable cards included in resources)
Sorting animals into nocturnal and flying. (photocopiable cards included in resources)

Figure 13.9 Ideas for practising sorting

Practise using the cause and effect, sequence and Venn diagrams to organise information from the children's current class topics. This will make the tools relevant and meaningful for them.

Chapter 14

Chunking

This chapter looks at chunking, providing:

- an explanation of the strategies;
- an optional script for delivering the sessions;
- games for practising chunking.

Chunking is breaking down information into smaller parts that are easier to retain. For example, when we say telephone numbers we automatically chunk them into sections; 01635219742 is difficult to remember as one long number, it is longer than the seven digits that most people can hold in their short-term memory. However, divided into 01635 219 742, most people will find it much easier to remember.

Optional script

Today we are going to look at a way to help you remember that is called chunking. Chunking involves grouping things to be remembered together into smaller chunks. Listen to this string of numbers: 219742. Can you remember what the numbers were? It is quite tricky to remember six numbers but if we break them into two groups 219 742, then remembering them will be easier. Can you remember them now? We may even be able to add another set of numbers and still remember them. Try this: 01635 219 742. This is how people remember phone numbers.

Memory club poster 7

Introduce memory club poster 7 – chunking. Give the children the information sheet for parents about chunking.

Games

Remembering telephone numbers

This is a repetition of the activity in the naming and rehearsal section, however, this time we are going to demonstrate to the children how chunking the numbers makes them easier to remember.

The adult reads out the list of telephone numbers and the children repeat each set of numbers. When the children have grasped the game increase the difficulty by:

1   asking the children to enter the numbers on a calculator;
2   writing the numbers on a whiteboard.

With both of these activities the children must not start entering the digits until the whole telephone number has been given, and the numbers are shown to each other and compared and checked after each digit. The difficulty can also be increased by lengthening the sequence of digits. Once the children cope well with the number of digits in the telephone number, move to the next level. The difficulty can also be increased by having a time lag in between giving the children the numbers and them writing them down or putting them into the computer.

Basic – four digits	Medium – five digits	Hard – six digits
92 40	864 81	541 938
27 39	941 27	396 627
94 83 etc	594 72 etc	393 272 etc

Figure 14.1 Remembering telephone numbers

Chinese whispers with numbers

Children sit in a line. Start by using the sequence of digits in Level 1 and move up the levels as the children get more skilled at using this strategy. Whisper the sequence of numbers to the first child in the line, chunking them as you say them. Write the sequence on a whiteboard where none of the children can see it. The numbers are then whispered from person to person until they reach the other end of the line. The person at the end of the line will write the numbers on a whiteboard and the two lists of numbers are compared.

Level 1 Four digits	Level 2 Five digits	Level 3 6 digits
4 7 – 8 3	5 9 1 – 8 5	8 5 – 7 1 – 0 7
2 9 – 5 8	2 9 5 – 4 7	3 8 – 1 9 – 7 5
7 3 – 4 0	8 9 8 – 3 2	4 7 – 9 3 – 7 1
2 9 – 0 5	9 3 8 – 5 9	9 4 – 7 2 – 7 5
Etc	Etc	

Figure 14.2 Examples of number strings at different levels

Chapter 15

Applying memory strategies

This chapter looks at memory strategies for learning:

- spelling;
- times tables.

Learning spellings and times tables can be a particular challenge for children with memory difficulties. This chapter looks at strategies that can be used to support these specific areas of learning.

Applying techniques to help with spellings

In this section we will look at a general approach to learning spelling and also at strategies for tricky words. Memory strategies are most useful for irregular words or words that a child is finding particularly difficult. It would be impossible for a child to have a memory aid to spell every word!

• To identify which words are 'troublemakers' and recognise the tricky parts.
• To apply a limited number of mnemonic devices.
• To build a personal resource list of words the child tends to misspell.
• To look for families of words with similar spelling patterns e.g. eight, neigh, weigh etc.

Figure 15.1 Useful skills for spelling

With this in mind the following skills are useful for the children to develop.
    Children will learn best if the method they are using is multi-sensory:

SIGHT – Motion, larger size and bright colours make SIGHT information easier to remember.
HEARING – listening to your teacher or other students in class; listening to CDs or other sources of sound information; listening to yourself as you read or speak.
MOTION – Receiving information into your brain through movements that your body makes. This can be whole body movements such as running or movements of small parts of your body as in writing or drawing. Speaking also involves moving parts of your body. Your brain will remember movements that you make time after time in the same way that a footpath will be worn if people walk the same way day after day.

TOUCH – Nerve endings in your fingertips and all over your skin can sense heat and cold, rough and smooth, and a variety of other textures and conditions. Ways to use TOUCH to help you learn or remember new information: write words with your fingertips in sand (or salt) spread over a large tray; use finger paints to write or draw new information; use textured letters (made of carpeting, plastic, wood, metal, etc.) to spell out words.

SPEECH – This can actually combine most of the other channels in one activity: the movement of your lips, tongue, cheeks, jaw, vocal cords, lungs; hearing the sounds of your speech; seeing words on a page if you are reading aloud; touch, if you follow along on the page with your finger while you read.

Multi-sensory strategy for learning spellings

The best way to use this approach with your group is to use this strategy for the children to learn their weekly spellings. Place the word you want to learn in front of you so you can see it easily. If you can, place the word up and to your left. It may sound silly but moving your eyes up and left has been shown to aid memory.

Figure 15.2 Moving your eyes can help memory

Close your eyes, and try to see the spelling of the word in your head. Open your eyes and look at the correct spelling again. Close your eyes and move them up and to the left and picture the correct spelling in your mind's eye. Say the letters you can see quietly to yourself. Open your eyes and look at the word. Then close your eyes and imagine the word again. Use your finger to 'write' the letters you can see in the air, on the table or on the floor.

Look at your mental image and then open your eyes and try to write down the letters that you can see. Check your spelling against the word you started with. If you have not spelt it correctly, repeat the process.

Helpful tips

Tips for using multi-sensory strategies for spelling:

- Make the word a distinctive colour.
- Make any letters that you are finding particularly difficult stand out in some way; make them bigger, bolder, brighter, a different colour or font.
- Break the word up into syllables and focus on one chunk at a time.
- If the word is a long one, make the letters small enough so that you can see the whole word together.
- For multi-syllabic words, make each syllable a different colour.

Picture/word association: visualisation and association

Research has shown that some children find it much easier to learn spellings if they associate each word with a picture while they are learning it. These can either be downloaded clipart pictures or ones that the child has drawn. What is important is that the child is involved in the selection of the picture – it needs to be meaningful to them if they are going to remember it. The children can annotate their weekly spelling list with their own pictures – which will serve to help them remember.

Memory strategies for 'tricky' words

Mnemonics

Mnemonics are devices that make spellings more interesting or distinctive and so help you to remember them. It would be impossible for a child to remember one of these for every word – they should be used only for tricky words that a child is struggling to remember.

Examples of spelling mnemonics

- Big elephants can always understand small elephants – because.
- Never eat crisps, eat salad sandwiches and remain young – necessary.
- Rhythm helps your two hips move – rhythm.
- I've got hairy tights – -ight endings.
- Sally Anne is dancing – said.
- Desert/dessert – remember that desert has s for sand in the middle, while dessert has two s's for sweet stuff.
- Here/hear – you hear with your ear.

Making pictures within the letters of words

This can be a powerful and fun way to help children with words they are finding difficult. Study the letters of the word that the child is having difficulty with and together create a picture using the shape of the letters. Again, it is important that the child is involved in the selection of the picture – it needs to be meaningful to them if they are going to remember it. See the example in the figure below.

The aim of all these different spelling memory strategies is that the child will use them as a support until the spelling of the word becomes automatic – most adults do not think about the spelling of every word they write.

Figure 15.3 Create a picture using the shape of the letters

Applying techniques to help with times tables

There are too many number facts for some children to recall when learning their tables – so the first thing to do is help them to make the most of what they do know. There is no need to memorise every single multiplication fact, we can help the children to reduce the amount of number facts they are trying to learn.

Every multiplication has a twin, as long as you understand that 6x8 = 8x6 there are fewer facts to learn. This way, you only have to remember half the table. Remembering square numbers down the diagonal can also help.

	1	2	3	4	5	6	7	8	9	10
1	1	2	3	4	5	6	7	8	9	10
2	2	4	6	8	10	12	14	16	18	20
3	3	6	9	12	15	18	21	24	27	30
4	4	8	12	16	20	24	28	32	36	40
5	5	10	15	20	25	30	35	40	45	50
6	6	12	18	24	30	36	42	48	54	60
7	7	14	21	28	35	42	49	56	63	70
8	8	16	24	32	40	48	56	64	72	80
9	9	18	27	36	45	54	63	72	81	90
10	10	20	30	40	50	60	70	80	90	100

Figure 15.4 Times tables table

Times table tricks

Some children find these useful, however, for some it just adds to what they need to remember. They may be useful if a child is finding one or two particular times tables difficult to master.

Times table	Trick
2	Add the number to itself (example 2×9 = 9+9)
5	The last digit always goes 5, 0, 5, 0, ..,
	is always half of 10× (Example: 5x6 = half of 10x6 = half of 60 = 30)
	is half the number times 10 (Example: 5x6 = 10x3 = 30)
6	If you multiply 6 by an even number, they both end in the same digit. Example: 6×**2** = 1**2**, 6×**4** = 2**4**, 6×**6** = 3**6**, etc.
9	The last digit always goes 9,8,7,6, ... Up to 10×9 the two digits in the answer always add up to a total of 9
	If you *add* the answer's digits together, you get 9. Example: 9×5 = 45 and 4+5 = 9. (But not with 9×11=99)
10	Put a zero after the number of 10s
11	Up to 9×11: just repeat the digit (Example: 4×11 = 44)

Figure 15.5 Times tables tricks

Using rhyme with times tables

Rhyme can also be used for some of those tricky-to-remember times tables facts. For example, 7 and 7 went down the line to capture number 49; 7 and 8 used lots of bricks to make house number 56; 8 and 4 made some stew and gave it to 32 (rhymes don't have to make sense!). The children can combine these with silly visual images to strengthen the memory.

Times tables songs and raps

There are lots of really useful times tables songs, chants and raps freely available on YouTube. They are often accompanied by great visuals. These songs, chants and raps combine the powerful effects of rhythm, music and visual images to help support memory. In addition to this, the children enjoy them and so hearing them several times gives the opportunity to revisit and overlearn the concepts.

Chapter 16

Review and application of strategies

This chapter looks at:

- reviewing of the strategies taught;
- choosing the most appropriate strategy for a task.

Reviewing strategies and choosing the best strategy for a task

Explain to the group that you have looked at all the memory strategies and that the important thing now is to be able to choose the best one to use for each situation. Using the mind map you created as a group, review all the different memory strategies the group have looked at.

Games

What helps me to remember? (with photocopiable page)

Look at the different statements on the cards to sort and discuss whether or not they are a useful memory strategy.

Memory challenges (with photocopiable page)

Take it in turns to pick a challenge card and think about the strategy that would be useful in each situation. Remember to stress that there is not one correct answer; everyone is different and different strategies will be more effective for different people.

Explain to the group that we are going to play a series of games and their challenge is to choose for themselves which memory strategy would be the most effective to play the game. Any of the games from the previous chapters can be re-used here, and there are also several new games below that can also be used.

After you have had several turns at each game, stop and ask the children what strategy they are using to help them to remember. Is their strategy working or does someone else have a strategy that may work better for them? Repeat the game after the discussion so that the children have a chance to experiment with an alternative strategy.

Shape sorter challenge (with photocopiable page)

Each player needs to have a set of the shapes cut out ready to use and a copy of the box from the photocopiable activities. Give instructions for selecting shapes and placing them in exact positions in the box. Gradually increase the number of items and the complexity of the instructions. The children should not start sorting the shapes or arranging them until all the instructions have been given. Asking them to put the page with the box printed on it face down on top of their shapes while you give the instructions will help stop them from doing this. Example instructions at different levels:

1   Choose a circle and a rectangle. Put the rectangle in the middle of the bottom side of the box. Put the circle in the bottom right-hand corner.
2   Choose two triangles and a hexagon. Put one triangle in the top right-hand corner and one triangle in the bottom left-hand corner. Put the hexagon in the middle of the box.
3   Choose two squares, a circle and a rectangle. Put the rectangle in the middle of the bottom side of the box. Put the circle on top of the rectangle. Put a square in each of the top corners.
4   Choose two rectangles. Two circles and a square. Put the square in the middle of the box. Put one circle above the square and one below. Put one rectangle to the left of the square and one to the right.

Cafe menu (with photocopiable page)

The children have a copy of the menu photocopy. They listen to the order and then have to mark the things ordered on their menu sheet. The challenge in the game can be increased by increasing the number of items ordered and the delay between hearing the items and recording on the sheet.

Cracking the safe (game 1) (with photocopiable page)

Prepare each of the children a copy of the cracking the safe sheet – if you laminate this you can reuse it like a whiteboard. The aim of the game is to correctly record the combination of numbers and letters that they are given as the safe combination. Start by giving combinations of four numbers and letters and build up to seven. The children should put their boards face down while the numbers are being called. The challenge can be increased by including a greater delay between hearing the combination and recording it.

Cracking the safe (game 2) (with photocopiable page)

Increase the difficulty of the task by giving the pupils the combination in the reverse order. For example, if the combination is 4, 6, d, 3 you tell them 3, d, 6, 4 and they must reverse it in their head before they write it down. As before, the challenge can be increased by increasing the number of items to be recalled and introducing a bigger time delay.

Word sorting

The aim of this game is for children to listen to a list of objects and then sort them by their physical attributes, for example, biggest to smallest, coldest to warmest, thickest to thinnest, etc. Start by using three objects to sort and as the children get more skilled add in one or two more.

I am going to read a list of words to you. I want you to listen carefully and then say them in order from smallest to largest. For example, if I were to say elephant, mouse, cow, you would say mouse, cow, elephant.

Table 16.1 Sorting from smallest to largest

Farm animals

Cow	Sheep	Chicken	
Duck	Horse	Goat	
Bull	Cat	Pigeon	

Pets

Guinea pig	Mouse	Dog	Cat
Stick insect	Horse	Rabbit	Dog
Gerbil	Parrot	Dog	Goldfish

Zoo animals

Leopard	Hummingbird	Hippo	Monkey
Rhino	Lion	Tree frog	Meerkat
Parrot	Elephant	Koala	Hyena

Fruits

Orange	Cherry	Watermelon	Raisin	Pineapple
Apple	Melon	Satsuma	Grapefruit	Grape
Plum	Watermelon	Kiwi fruit	Blueberry	Orange

Table 16.2 Sorting from tallest to shortest

House	Sky scraper	Doll's house	Bungalow
Mouse	Giraffe	Dog	Tiger
Bush	Flower	Grass	Tree

Table 16.3 Sorting from lightest to heaviest

Ping pong ball	Bowling ball	Football
Watermelon	Grape	Apple
Elephant	Fly	Monkey
Plane	Bike	Car

Table 16.4 Sorting from thickest to thinnest

Arm	Tree trunk	Finger
Elephant	Stick insect	Monkey
Piece of paper	Book	Wall
Needle	Rope	Man

Table 16.5 Sorting from coldest to warmest

Jam sandwich	Ice cream	Soup	
Spring	Winter	Summer	
Lava	Sand	Snow	
Desert	Ice berg	Bath water	Classroom
Hot chocolate	Tap water	Slush puppy	Bath water

Table 16.6 Sorting from longest to shortest

Train	Truck	Motorbike	
Arm	Hand	Finger	
Twig	Branch	Tree	
Paper clip	Pencil	Skipping rope	
Goldfish	Shark	Whale	
Crayon	Ruler	Pencil	Metre stick
A morning	An hour	A minute	A day
A day	A century	A month	A year

In the bag (with photocopiable page)

Fill a feely bag with one of the sets of pictures (for example, zoo animals). The group sits together and the adult starts by selecting a card from the bag and says, 'I went to the zoo and saw a penguin.' The penguin card is then placed face-up in the middle of the table. The next player takes a card and says, 'I went to the zoo and I saw a penguin and an elephant.' The elephant card is placed face-up on top of the other card. The game continues until all the cards have been taken from the bag, or when the memory load is beyond the capacity of the children playing.

Discuss with the children the useful strategies they could use to help them. This may be checking off the items in their fingers, looking at the person who said the items and associating the words with them, repeating the items in their heads. This is a co-operative game rather than a competitive one, if a child cannot think of a word in the list the other players can give clues to help trigger their memory.

Picture sets available as photocopiable pages: at the beach, at school, at the zoo.

Measuring impact

At the end of the programme it is important to repeat the baseline measure that was taken before the programme started so that you can measure the impact the programme has had, and also to identify if there are any future areas of development for the children.

Chapter 17

Resources

Working memory checklist

Organisational skills/attention and concentration

Fails to follow multi-step instructions ☐

Tends to lose their belongings ☐

Has difficulty keeping their place in a complex task with multiple steps ☐

Struggles with activities that combine storing and processing information ☐

Has difficulty maintaining attention and staying on task ☐

Appears to be lacking in motivation ☐

Appears to be inattentive ☐

Is easily distracted especially when working on something that is not of interest to them ☐

Shows poor attention to detail ☐

Has difficulty getting started on a piece of work ☐

Has difficulty when planning something that needs to be done in separate steps ☐

Has difficulty in integrating new information with prior knowledge ☐

When chosen to answer a question forgets what he/she wanted to say ☐

Has difficulty staying on task when tasks are cognitively demanding, but attends well when cognitive demands of the task are minimal ☐

Has trouble waiting his/her turn; for example, in a conversation or when asking for help ☐

Benefits from teacher support to stay on task and complete longer tasks ☐

Does not carry out classroom instructions accurately, i.e. will complete some but not all steps of an instruction ☐

Forgets how to continue an activity they have started ☐

Unable to explain what they should be doing during an activity ☐

Has normal social relationships with his/her peers ☐

Is reserved in group activities ☐

Has difficulty delivering a verbal message accurately ☐

Has difficulties in literacy ☐

Has difficulty remembering a story in sequence ☐

Has difficulty remembering their place in a sentence or paragraph they are writing ☐

Has difficulty in understanding and following a story they are reading ☐

Has difficulty in remembering grammatical rules ☐

Has difficulty in note-taking or copying from the board ☐

Has difficulty taking notes and listening at the same time ☐

Difficulties in numeracy

Is inconsistent in remembering maths facts ☐

Has difficulty in learning and retrieving mathematical facts and applying them in problem solving ☐

Has difficulty remembering a sequence of four or more numbers ☐

Has difficulty with problems that require holding information in mind, for example, mental maths calculations ☐

Exhibits slow information retrieval ☐

Has difficulty learning mathematical procedures ☐

Short-term memory baseline assessments 1–8

Pupil record form

Child's name _____   Date of assessment _____

Task	Child's initial score	Child's final score
Listen to the numbers that I call out – can you repeat the sequence back to me?	— 10	— 10
Listen to the numbers that I call out – can you repeat the sequence back to me in the reverse order, i.e. give me the last number first? The sequences will increase in length.	— 10	— 10
Study the card with 20 pictures on it for 30 seconds. Cover the sheet. How many can you remember in any order?	— 20	— 20
Look at the card with a line of 10 digits on it for 30 seconds. How many of the numbers can you remember in the correct order?	— 10	— 10
Look at the card with a line of 10 shapes on it for 30 seconds. How many of the numbers can you remember in the correct order?	— 10	— 10
Listen to the list of colours I give you, then turn over your page and colour the strip of boxes in those colours in the same order you heard them.	— 20	— 20
Look at the grid and study the position of the different coloured squares for 30 seconds.	— 10	— 10
Look at the grid and try to remember the position of the dots. Cover the grid and try to draw the dots on the blank copy.	— 10	— 10
Total score	— 100	— 100

Baseline assessment task 1

Digits to repeat in the same order	
3, 7, 6	
4, 9, 7	
6, 2, 9, 5	
9, 4, 2, 8	
2, 5, 8, 1, 0	
3, 7, 1, 8, 4	
7, 1, 4, 2, 9, 0	
5, 2, 7, 9, 1, 6	
3, 6, 1, 8, 4, 8, 6	
5, 1, 7, 9, 3, 6, 4	
Total number of correct sequences	

Baseline assessment task 2

Digits to repeat in reverse order		
Sequence	Correct response	
2, 5, 9	9, 5, 2	
6, 1, 8	8, 1, 6	
3, 7, 4, 9	9, 4, 7, 3	
5, 9, 3, 6	6, 3, 9, 5	
3, 6, 4, 9, 7	7, 9, 4, 6, 3	
8, 2, 5, 7, 4	4, 7, 5, 2, 8	
9, 1, 4, 6, 8, 2	2, 8, 6, 4, 1, 9	
7, 1, 3, 5, 9, 4	4, 9, 5, 3, 1, 7	
9, 1, 5, 8, 3, 5, 7	7, 5, 3, 8, 5, 1, 9	
1, 6, 9, 3, 7, 4, 8	8, 4, 7, 3, 9, 6, 1	
Total number of correct sequences		

Baseline assessment task 3: record sheet

Child's name _____   Date of assessment _____

Butterfly		Grapes	
Chick		Sun	
Elephant		Strawberry	
Heart		Flag	
Fish		Snowman	
Kite		Umbrella	
Apple		Ladybird	
Trumpet		Pencil	
Paint box		Star	
Watch		Key	

Baseline assessment task 4: record sheet

Cross through numbers correctly name in the right sequence by the pupil

6839243178

Total number correctly remembered

Baseline assessment task 5: record sheet

Cross through shapes correctly name in the right sequence by the pupil

Total number correctly remembered

Baseline assessment task 3

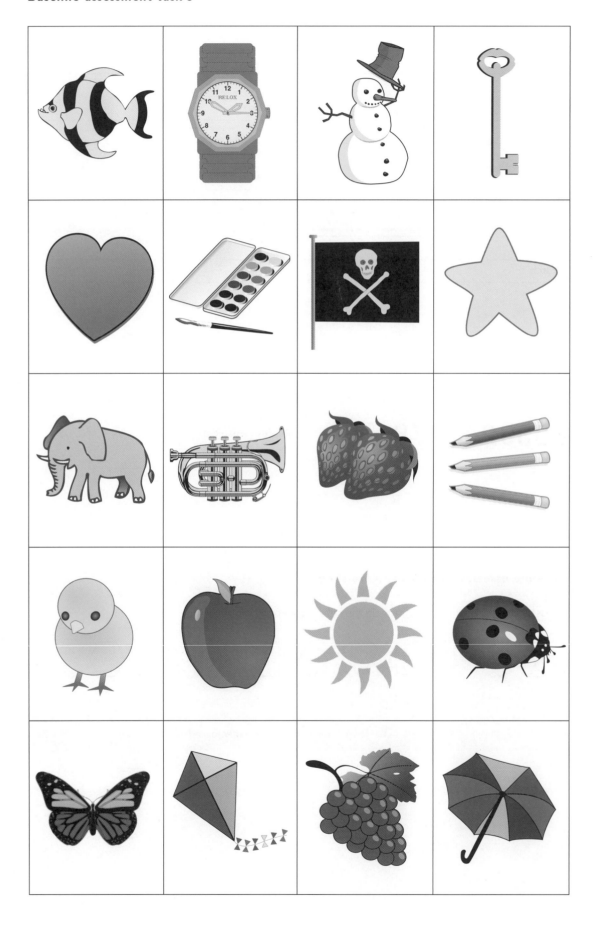

Baseline assessment task 4

6 8 3 9 2 4 3 1 7 8

Baseline assessment task 5

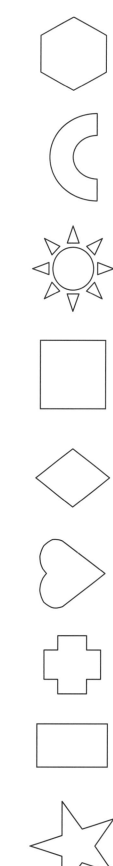

Baseline assessment task 6 – pupil response sheet

Pupil sheet			
1.			
2.			
3.			
4.			

Baseline assessment task 7 – pupil response sheet

Pupil sheet

Baseline assessment task 7

red			blue	
	yellow	red		red
yellow			blue	
			yellow	
blue				blue

Baseline assessment task 8

●			
			●

		●	
●			

		●	
	●		

●		●	

		●	●
	●		

Baseline assessment task 8 – pupil response sheet

Parent consent letter

Dear Parents,

This term we will be running a programme for pupils, that aims to enable the children to make the best use of their short-term memory by learning and using memory strategies. The programme will run for three short sessions each week and will work on the following objectives:

1 the acquisition of memory strategies;
2 the maximisation of memory capacity by implementing the following strategies inside and outside the intervention sessions; naming, rehearsing, visualisation, linking, chunking and grouping;
3 enhancing the children's confidence and self-esteem.

During the course we will keep parents informed about which strategy the children are currently working on, and provide some short home-based activities, so that the work of the group can be consolidated at home. These home-based tasks will also encourage the children to use their memory strategies at home as well as in school.

This group will be run by _____ in close consultation with the SENCo _____.

Your child's teacher has suggested that they may be able to benefit from working in this group. Any additional support within school needs formal written permission from parents. Therefore, if you are happy for your child to take part in this enjoyable group, please complete and return the form below.

If you have any further questions please do not hesitate to contact me,

I give permission for my child_____ to take part in the memory club during the _____term.

Signed_____ date _____

Advice for parents

Short-term memory

This is where we store information on a temporary basis. Up to seven pieces of information can be retained for a short period of time. This is the memory we use for remembering a telephone number, a shopping list, a series of directions or instructions, or a list of jobs we have to do. By implementing specific memory strategies the performance of the short-term memory can be enhanced. That is the focus of the strategies of this course.

Working memory

This is the term used to describe the ability we have to hold in mind and mentally manipulate information over a short period of time. In this case we are not simply remembering and repeating the same information, but are doing something with it. A good example of when we use our working memory is mental arithmetic; for example, when we multiply 43 and 27 together without using a piece of paper. Without working memory we would not be able to carry out this type of complex mental activity in which we have to both keep in mind some information while processing other material.

Long-term memory

The long-term memory is a vast store that holds learned knowledge and past experiences and contains everything we know that is not currently being used but can be retrieved. It is estimated that only 1 per cent of information that passes into our consciousness will pass into our long-term memory. Once information reaches our long-term memory it can be retained for an entire lifetime, although some pieces of information decay over time.

The following guidelines may help to increase a child's short term within the home:

1 Ensure that the child is looking at you and listening to you before you give instructions.
2 Keep verbal instructions and important pieces of information clear and precise. Break down instructions into manageable chunks, and give instructions in the order you want your child to complete them.
3 Do not overload your child with too many pieces of information in one go – this will lead to memory failure.
4 Encourage your child to repeat the key pieces of information from the instructions before they start to follow them.
5 Be prepared to repeat the instructions/information if necessary.
6 Encourage your child to use the techniques they are learning in the memory club when they are at home to help them remember. You will be sent regular information sheets to keep you up to date with the strategies that your child is learning.
7 Reassure your child that it is acceptable to forget things from time to time – as we all do! Make a point of sharing your own memory failures with your child to help them realise that it happens to everyone.
8 Praise your child's successes – however small.

Parent information sheets 1–8

1 Naming and rehearsal

The memory strategy your child is currently working on in the memory club is naming and rehearsal.

This technique involves the repetition of words, either silently to yourself (rehearsal) or quietly out loud (naming) so that they are more easily remembered. This is useful for remembering telephone numbers, lists of objects you need to go and collect, etc.

The children will be starting with a small string of objects to remember and will work up to remembering longer strings.

It will help the children to begin to use this technique automatically if you also encourage them to use it at home, for example, when giving them a list of things they need to do to get ready for school/bed.

Counting items is helpful as a target to know how many items we need to remember and it can help trigger recall. If you have to remember four things but can only remember three, knowing you need one more and going over the task of checking it off on your fingers can act as a trigger to either recall the item or ask for help to remember it. The children will be encouraged to check items off on their fingers.

There are a number of free online resources that can help your child to practise naming and rehearsal skills.

Memory IV game

The children have to memorise the sequence of objects shown and then repeat the sequence by clicking on the objects. The game starts with a short sequence which is extended as the children successfully reproduce the sequence.

http://thekidzpage.com/freekidsgames/games/ngames/memory4/memory4-game.html

Celebrity Simon

There are nine different famous people, each of whom make a different funny noise. The game gives a sequence of celebrities/noises and the child has to repeat this in the same sequence by clicking on the picture of the celebrity. Just as in the traditional Simon game the sequence of noises to repeat gets longer and longer until the player makes a mistake.

http://thekidzpage.com/freekidsgames/games/celebrity_simon/simon-online-game.html

Trolley dash

In this game the children are given a shopping list (with pictures as well as words). They then have to go along the supermarket conveyor belt and click on all the items in their shopping list before the shopping time runs out. The time limit makes this quite challenging, so this game is best for children who have good mouse control.

http://gamesgames.com/game/Trolley_Dash.html

Parent information sheets 1–8 *Continued*

2 Visualisation

The memory strategy your child is currently working on in the memory club is visualisation.

Visualisation is using the technique of making mental images to aid memory. It involves making a mental picture in your head so that you can remember it. When we make an internal visual image of information we have heard it helps us to remember it.

The children will be encouraged to use mental images to help them remember information for the games we will be playing in school. The children will be starting with a small string of objects to remember and working up to remembering longer strings.

It will help the children to begin to use this technique automatically if you also encourage them to use it at home, for example, when giving them a list of things they need to do to get ready for school/bed. So rather than repeating the list of jobs to themselves they make a mental picture of each one.

Different people find that certain techniques work better for them than others. If your child is showing a strong preference for a certain technique and is resistant to trying another, don't try to push them – as long as they are remembering the things on their to-do list.

There are a number of free online resources that can help your child to practise spotting the key features in pictures.

Mental training – visual challenge – odd one out

In this game you simply have to click on the person who is different from the other three. The game starts simply by asking the children to spot very obvious differences, but as they succeed the difference become far more difficult to spot and they will need to look very closely to find them.

http://gamesgames.com/game/Mental-Training---Visual-Challenge.html

Mental training – visual challenge – odd one out – geometric shapes (dis-symmetry)

In this game you simply have to click on the shape that is different from the other three. The game starts by asking the children to spot very obvious differences, but as they succeed the differences become far more difficult to spot and they will need to look very closely to find them. The game also makes it more difficult to spot the differences by putting the shape into different orientations. This game is more difficult that the person game on the same web site.

http://gamesgames.com/game/Mental-Training---Visual-Challenge.html

I lost my puppy

This game involves studying a 'photograph' of a missing dog and then identifying that dog from the other dogs in the park. The game starts simply by asking the children to distinguish between just two very different dogs in the park, however, it gradually becomes more difficult as they succeed by making the dogs more similar, and introducing more dogs to choose from.

http://gamesgames.com/game/i-lost-my-puppy.html

Find the suspect

This game presents you with a number of faces to memorise. Starting with just one and increasing in number if you are successful. These target faces then disappear and you then have to identify the 'suspect' from the new faces you are shown. This game is made easier if you focus on the key distinctive features of each face.

http://thekidzpage.com/freekidsgames/games/nggames/suspect-game1.html

Parent letter 2 (accompanies information sheet 2)

Dear Parents,

Today we began to use the strategy of visualisation to help remember things. This is the explanation and activity that your child was given: 'We often need to remember to do things that are not that interesting and so are not easy to remember, e.g. give a note to your mum. However, if we use our imagination to make the picture in our head of what we need to do more interesting, then we can make it more exciting and easier to remember. If we add imaginary smells, sensations and noises we make the image even more memorable.'

For example, imagine that you need to remember to post an important letter. First, picture the ordinary envelope, and then change this picture to make it more interesting and memorable. For example, picture yourself staggering along the road with an enormous golden envelope. The envelope is decorated with sparkling, flashing red stars. It smells of chocolate and is making a mooing noise like a cow. The envelope feels freezing cold and your fingers are chilly.

Each child has been given a letter in an envelope that they have been asked to give to their parents tonight. Each child was given time to develop their own personal memory story to help them to remember to deliver the letter. They were reminded to include imaginary smells, sensations and noises, and given time to share their memory stories with the group. At the end of the session the children were sent to put the letters into their school bags so that they would have to remember them at the end of the day.

Hopefully your child will have remembered to give you this! It will help to reinforce what they have been doing if you ask them to explain the strategy to you and share their memory story. In future, if you are sending anything into school for your child to give in, please encourage them to use this technique to help them to remember to give it in. They will benefit far more from the memory club if they are encouraged to use what they are learning at home as well as at school.

Thank you.

Parent information sheets 1–8 *Continued*

3 Keywords for meaning

Keywords are the main ideas in a message. When we talk, much of what we say is not needed. For example, 'Look at the time, it's getting late, if we don't hurry we are going to be late for school. Hurry up and go and clean your teeth and brush your hair. Make sure you have put your reading book in your school bag and don't forget your lunchbox.'

Here the keywords are in italics: 'Look at the time, it's getting late, if we don't *hurry* we are going to be late for school. Hurry up and go and clean your *teeth* and brush your *hair*. Make sure you have put your *reading book* in your school bag and don't forget your *lunchbox*.'

This links back to both rehearsal and visualisation, because it is really only the keywords that need to be rehearsed or visualised. It is only essential that this important information is remembered – anything else is a bonus!

Just as focusing on the keywords can help to remember verbal information, focusing on the key pictures will help to remember visual information. It will really help your child with both of these techniques if you help them to isolate the keywords they need to remember.

Once your child has become confident with using the techniques of repetition and visualisation we will be encouraging them to experiment with using both at the same time since they can use more than one strategy at a time to help then to remember.

Parent information sheets 1–8 *Continued*

4 Chaining and linking

The memory strategy your child is currently working on in the memory club is chaining and linking.

Association or linking ideas helps children to remember information because it helps them to group it together. One way of linking is to use categories and put the objects from the same categories together. For example, if trying to remember a shopping list – apples, banana and oranges would go together, as would yoghurts, milk and butter. Another way of using chaining is to link items that need to be remembered from different categories together using a silly story or picture; this is the example the children were given in school:

The words we are trying to remember are: elephant, swimming pool, golden crown, fish and chips, helicopter and mountain.

> One day a large grey *elephant* went for a dip at the *swimming pool*. He dived down to the bottom of the pool and found a *golden crown*. He picked it up and wore it home. On the way home he was very hungry after all his swimming so he had *fish and chips* for tea. Then he was tired so he could not walk any further and so he got a *helicopter* back to his *mountain* home.

Yet another way is to link the information to be remembered to something you already know – this could be a memory, character, song, rhyme or rhythm or a piece of information. Lots of adults use this strategy without even realising it. For example, if I remember the date 12 May, by remembering that it is the month before my birthday (April) and the digits are reversed (12 instead of 21). Or if I set the PIN code for a credit card to the phone number or birthday of a friend or relative.

Some people find that linking words to be remembered to a rhythm aids their memory – a bit like a rap! Other people find that putting lists of words to be remembered into a favourite song and singing them to themselves aids their memory.

Mnemonics

A useful way of trying to remember information is simply playing with the first letters of words to make a sentence to help you remember. This works by making the information you want to remember more memorable and is particularly useful for remembering information in a particular order. All you do is take the first letter of each word you want to learn and make another word. Well known mnemonics include:

- Richard of York gave battle in vain: for remembering the sequence of the colours of the rainbow – red, orange, yellow, green, blue, indigo, violet.
- Never eat shredded wheat – for remembering the points of the compass – north, south, east, and west.
- My very easy method just speeds up names for naming planets in order – Mercury, Venus, Earth, Mars, Jupiter, Saturn, Uranus, Neptune.

Parent information sheets 1–8 *Continued*

5 Visualisation and linking

Linking two strategies can add to the impact they have on your memory. Encourage the children to start making a mental picture of the associations they are making to support their memory.

The journey system – this links together the skills of visualisation and association and is useful for remembering a list of information.

Start by using a familiar journey. We can use this journey to help us to remember a list of objects by imagining that we are walking through this familiar place and we see the objects on our list at certain point along the way.

When the children are introduced to this method at school they will be given the challenge of trying to remember a list of 13 objects in order. They will also be encouraged to try to remember this list and tell it to you when they come home.

Parent information sheets 1–8 *Continued*

6 Visual organisers for information

Organising information and sorting it into a diagram can be a very useful memory tool. The act of sorting makes the pupils look at, and think about the material, and also helps to make sure that they fully understand it, which in itself will support memory. In addition, organising information in a visual way can be a powerful memory tool. These tools help pupils to see things that they are trying to learn and help to organise information. There are many different types of visual organisation strategies.

Mind maps

Mind maps work well because they use several memory tools, including visual images, imagination and association. Mind maps use words, phrases and pictures to record ideas and include lines to organise these ideas into areas and to show the connections between these different areas.

Lots of examples of mind maps are freely available on the Internet, try typing mind map into Google and asking your child to tell you what they know about mind maps. Other types of mind map are listed below.

Cause and effect diagrams

The boxes for a mind map can be organised to show cause and effect. The cause and effect design, with the event in the middle box, the causes listed in the boxes on the left and the effects listed in the boxes on the right. (The effects and the causes are connected to the event by lines.)

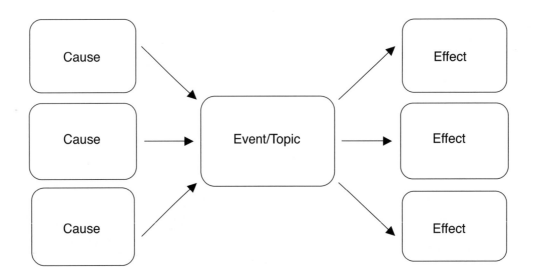

Sequencing diagrams

The boxes on a mind maps can be organised to show the order of a sequence of events. This can be really useful for sequencing a story of a recount of events.

Venn diagrams

Venn diagrams are very useful for comparing and contrasting two related areas of knowledge, with similarities between the two areas being in the middle section and difference in the outer areas.

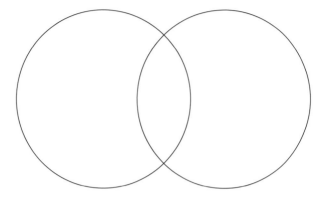

Parent information sheets I–8 *Continued*

7 Chunking

The memory strategy your child is currently working on in the memory club is chunking.

Chunking is where information is broken down into smaller parts that are easier to retain. For example, when we say telephone numbers we automatically chunk them into sections; 01635219742 is difficult to remember as one long number, it is longer than the seven digits that most people can hold in their short-term memory. However, divided into 01635 219 742, most people will find it much easier to remember.

You can help your child to practise this skill by encouraging them to remember and repeat telephone numbers to you.

Parent information sheets 1–8 *Continued*

8 Applying techniques to help with times tables

The memory club is currently working on applying the techniques they have been working on to help them with learning their times tables.

There are too many number facts for some children to recall when learning their tables – so the first thing to do is to help them to make the most of what they do know. There is no need to memorise every single multiplication fact. First, help the children to reduce the amount of number facts they are trying to learn.

Every multiplication has a twin, as long as you understand that 6x8 = 8x6 there are fewer facts to learn. This way, you only have to remember half the table. Remembering square numbers down the diagonal can also help.

Times tables table										
	1	2	3	4	5	6	7	8	9	10
1	1	2	3	4	5	6	7	8	9	10
2	2	4	6	8	10	12	14	16	18	20
3	3	6	9	12	15	18	21	24	27	30
4	4	8	12	16	20	24	28	32	36	40
5	5	10	15	20	25	30	35	40	45	50
6	6	12	18	24	30	36	42	48	54	60
7	7	14	21	28	35	42	49	56	63	70
8	8	16	24	32	40	48	56	64	72	80
9	9	18	27	36	45	54	63	72	81	90
10	10	20	30	40	50	60	70	80	90	100

Times tables tricks

Some children find these useful, however, for some it just adds to what they need to remember. They may be useful if a child is finding one or two particular times tables difficult to master.

Times table	Trick
2	Add the number to itself (example 2 x 9 = 9 + 9)
5	The last digit always goes 5, 0, 5, 0 . . .
	Is always half of 10x (example: 5 x 6 = half of 10 x 6 = half of 60 = 30)
	Is half the number times 10 (example: 5 x 6 = 10 x 3 = 30)
6	If you multiply 6 by an even number, they both end in the same digit (example: 6 x 2 = 12, 6 x 4 = 24, 6 x 6 = 36, etc.)
9	The last digit always goes 9, 8, 7, 6 . . .
	Up to 10 x 9 the two digits in the answer always add up to a total of 9
	If you *add* the answer's digits together, you get 9
	Example: 9 x 5 = 45 and 4 + 5 = 9. (But not with 9 x 11 = 99)
10	Put a zero after the number of 10s
11	Up to 9 x 11: just repeat the digit (example: 4 x 11 = 44)

Using rhyme with times tables

Rhyme can also be used for some of those tricky to remember times tables facts. For example, 7 and 7 went down the line to capture number 49; 7 and 8 used lots of bricks to make house number 56; 8 and 4 made some stew and gave it to 32 (rhymes don't have to make sense!). The children can combine these with silly visual images to strengthen the memory.

Times tables songs and raps

There are lots of really useful times tables songs, chants and raps freely available on YouTube. They are often accompanied by great visuals. These songs, chants and raps combine the powerful effects of rhythm, music and visual images to help support memory. In addition to this children will listen to them several times, giveing opportunity to revisit and learn the times tables.

Memory club posters 1–7

Memory club poster 1

Memory club posters 1–7 *Continued*

Memory club poster 2

Say it!

Say it!

Say it!

and

Remember

Memory club posters 1–7 *Continued*

Memory club poster 3

Make a picture in your head ...
... and remember what's been said!

Memory club posters 1–7 *Continued*

Memory club poster 4

The Key is to See.

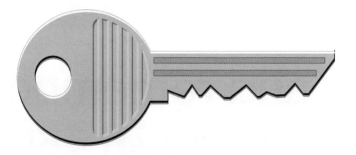

Hunt for the keyword ... ... and remember what you heard!

Memory club posters 1–7 *Continued*

Memory club poster 5

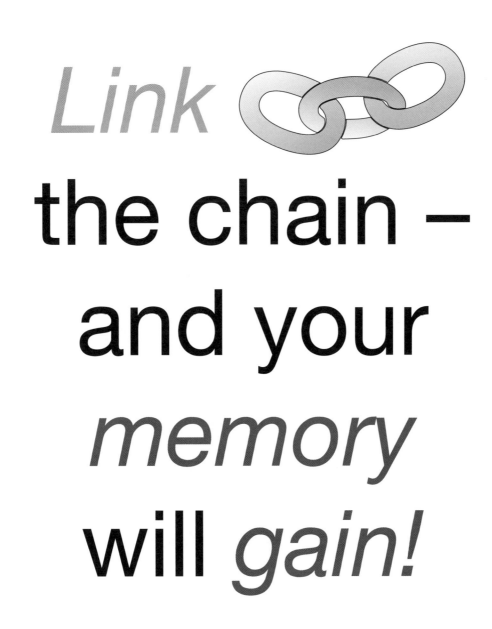

Memory club posters 1–7 *Continued*

Memory club poster 6

Sorting ideas on a chart ...

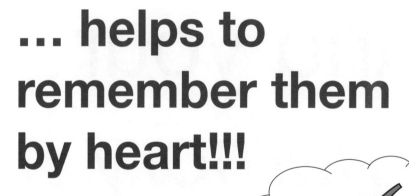

... helps to remember them by heart!!!

Memory club posters 1–7 *Continued*

Memory club poster 7

Chunk

01223712273

if you can – it's a *good* plan!

01223 71 22 73

List of games and activities

Activity	Strategy	Page number for explanatory notes	Resources
Listen and do	Listening skills	18	None needed
Copy me	Listening skills	18	None needed
Listen and draw	Listening skills	19	Photocopiable page
Treasure hunt	Naming and rehearsal	26	Photocopiable page
Countdown	Naming and rehearsal	27	None needed
Spot the missing word	Naming and rehearsal	27	None needed
Telephone numbers	Naming and rehearsal	27	None needed
Colouring grids	Naming and rehearsal	28	Photocopiable page
Remember this	Naming and rehearsal	28	Photocopiable page
Delete the number	Naming and rehearsal	29	Photocopiable page
Crazy cooks	Naming and rehearsal	30	Photocopiable page
Moving day	Naming and rehearsal	30	Photocopiable page
Phone factory	Naming and rehearsal	31	Photocopiable page
Using your imagination to the full	Visualisation	33	None needed
Driving through a picture	Visualisation	34	Use pictures available in school
Storytelling	Visualisation	34	None needed
Making memory movies	Visualisation	34	None needed
Magic potions	Visualisation and repetition	36	Photocopiable page
Listening for keywords	Keywords for meaning	39	None needed
Remember the treasure	Keywords and visualisation	40	Photocopiable page
Deep sea diver	Keywords and visualisation	41	Photocopiable page
Storytime	Keywords and visualisation	41	None needed
I went shopping	Chaining and linking	45	None needed
My favourite things	Chaining and linking	45	None needed
Sort the stuff	Chaining and linking	45	Use selection of pictures from other games
Storytelling	Chaining and linking	45	None needed
Song words	Chaining and linking	46	None needed
Rhyming	Chaining and linking	46	None needed
Drumming	Chaining and linking	47	None needed
Mnemonics	Chaining and linking	47	None needed
The journey	Visualisation and linking	48	None needed
Cause and effect diagrams	Visual organisers for information	53	Photocopiable page
Cause and effect sorting cards	Visual organisers for information	54	Photocopiable page
Sequence diagrams	Visual organisers for information	54	Photocopiable page
Venn diagrams	Visual organisers for information	54	Photocopiable page
Football teams and their kits	Visual organisers for information	54	Photocopiable page
Animals	Visual organisers for information	54	Photocopiable page
Remembering telephone numbers	Chunking	56	Individual whiteboards
Chinese whispers with numbers	Chunking	57	Individual whiteboards
What helps me to remember?	Review and application of strategies	63	Photocopiable page
Memory challenges	Review and application of strategies	63	Photocopiable page
Shape sorter challenge	Review and application of strategies	63	Photocopiable page
Cafe menu	Review and application of strategies	64	Photocopiable page
Cracking the safe	Review and application of strategies	64	Photocopiable page
Word sorting	Review and application of strategies	64	None needed
In the bag (at the beach)	Review and application of strategies	66	Photocopiable page
In the bag (at school)	Review and application of strategies	66	Photocopiable page
In the bag (at the zoo)	Review and application of strategies	66	Photocopiable page

Chapter 18

Photocopiable pages for games and activities

Listen and draw

1.	2.
3.	4.
5.	6.
7.	8.

Treasure hunt/Deep sea diver

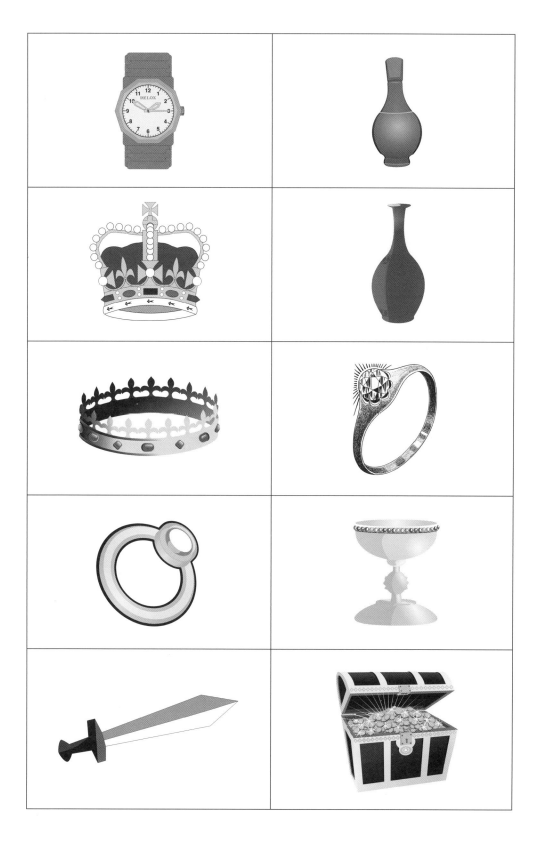

Colouring grids

Answer 1						
Answer 2						
Answer 3						
Answer 4						
Answer 5						
Answer 6						
Answer 7						
Answer 8						
Answer 9						
Answer 10						
Answer 11						
Answer 12						
Answer 13						
Answer 14						
Answer 15						

Remember this!

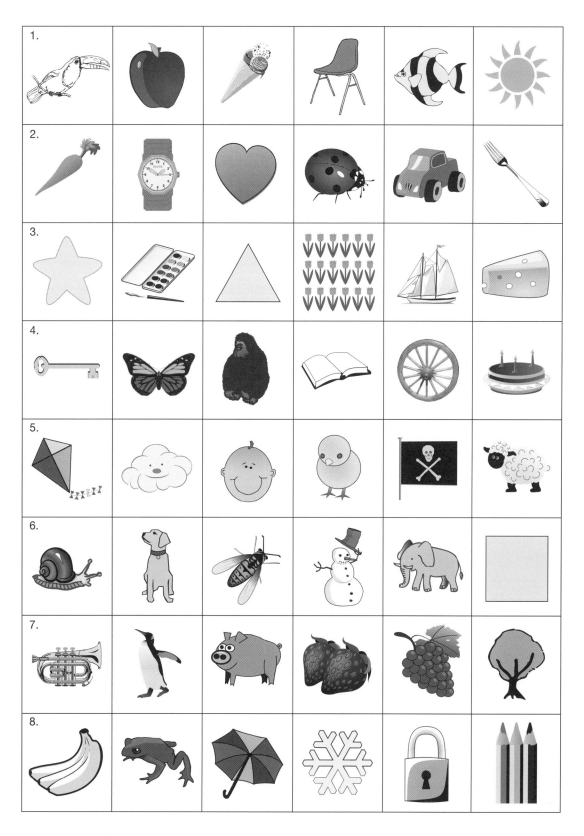

Delete the number: pupil sheet

a				
7	5	2	3	0
8	4	1	6	9
b				
1	9	7	5	3
0	4	6	8	2
c				
7	6	1	3	1
9	0	2	4	5
d				
8	1	5	6	9
0	7	4	3	2
e				
4	7	8	6	9
3	2	5	1	0
f				
9	8	1	5	6
2	7	4	3	0
g				
3	5	2	1	7
4	0	6	9	8
h				
7	4	5	2	6
9	3	1	1	0
i				
4	9	5	2	7
0	3	6	1	8
j				
6	1	2	5	7
4	0	9	8	3
k				
3	1	6	7	9
4	5	2	0	8
l				
1	4	6	3	7
5	0	2	0	9
m				
2	0	5	7	1
1	4	3	8	6
n				
0	4	5	6	8
1	7	3	2	9
o				
4	2	3	8	0
1	9	5	7	6

Crazy cooks

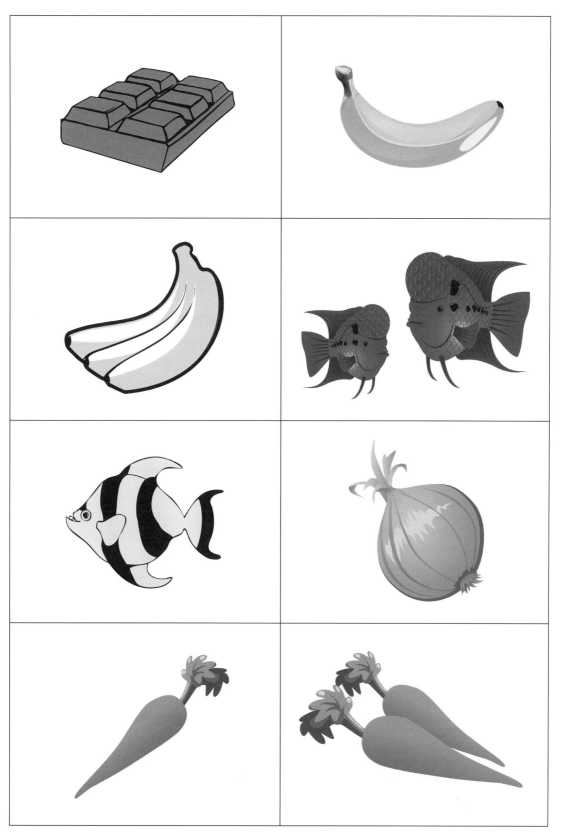

Crazy cooks *Continued*

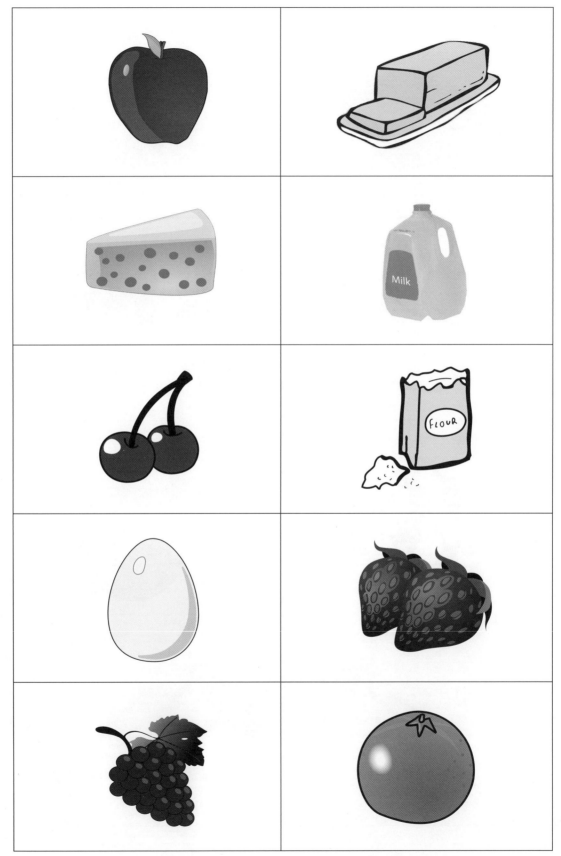

Moving day

Ground floor

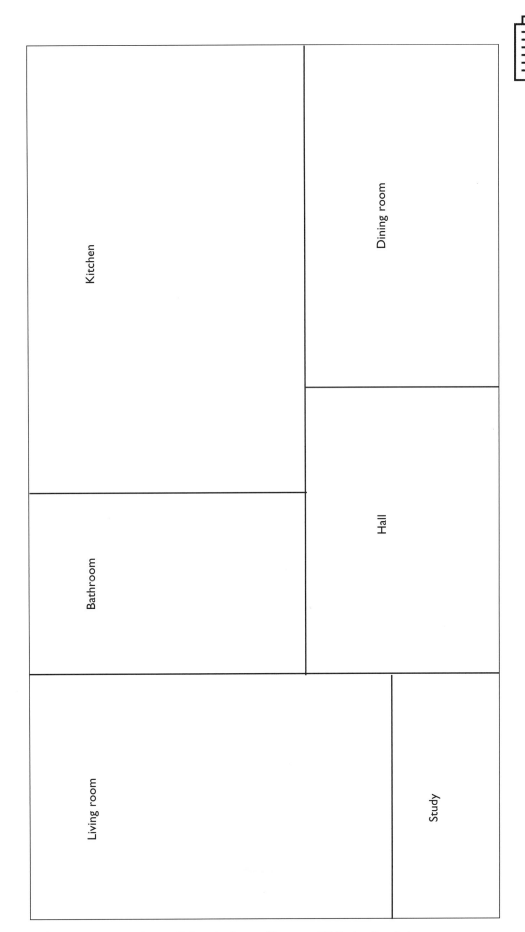

Kitchen

Dining room

Bathroom

Hall

Living room

Study

First floor

Bedroom 2

Bedroom 3

Bathroom

Landing

Bedroom 1

Bedroom 4

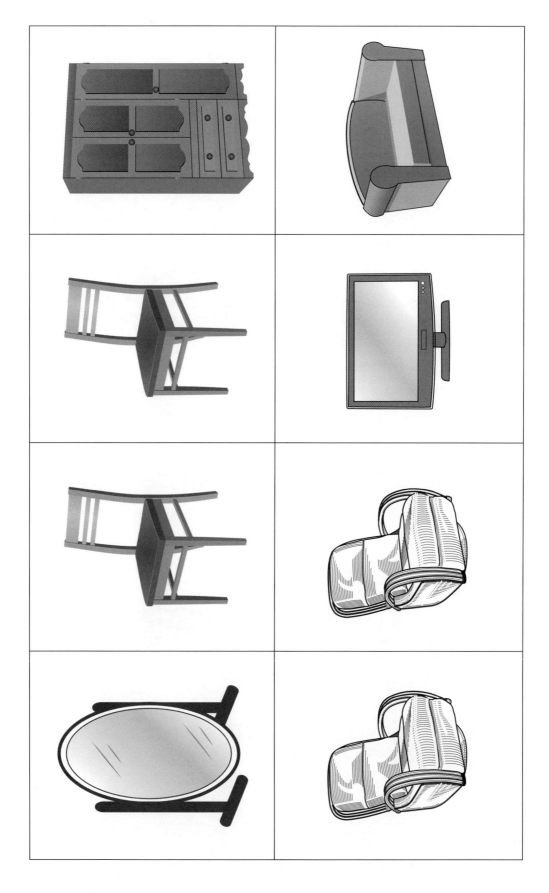

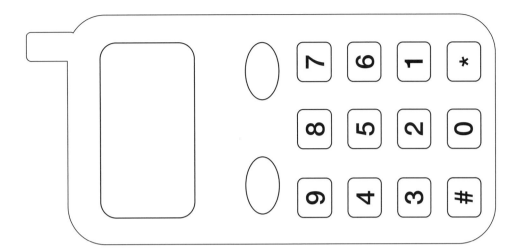

Phone factory

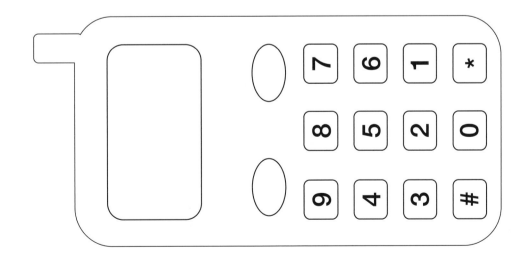

Magic potions

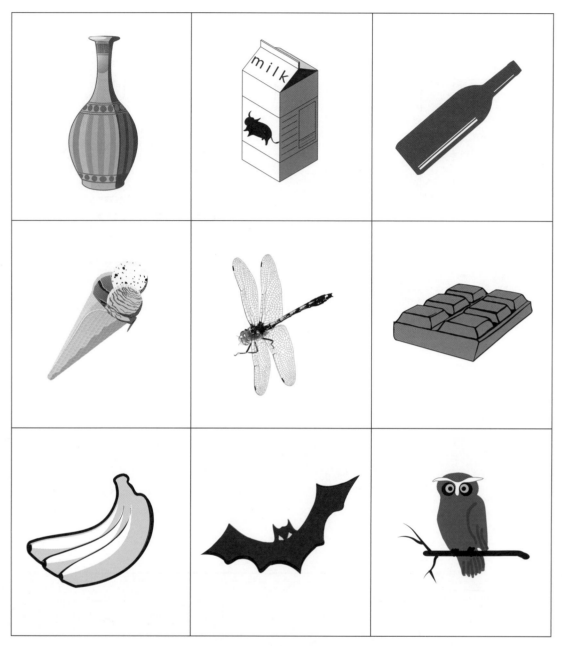

The Special Box

The lid of the box

The front of the box

Remember the treasure *Continued*

The bottle from under the sea

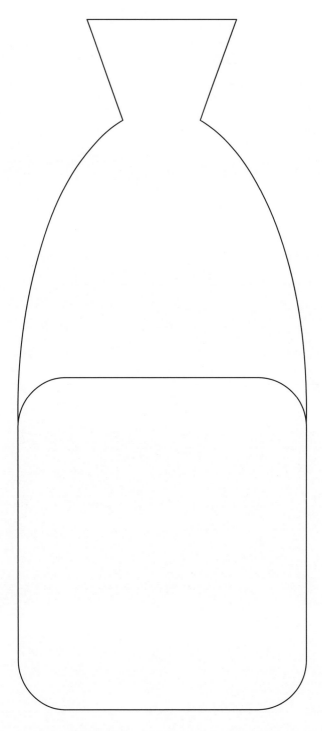

Cause and effect diagram

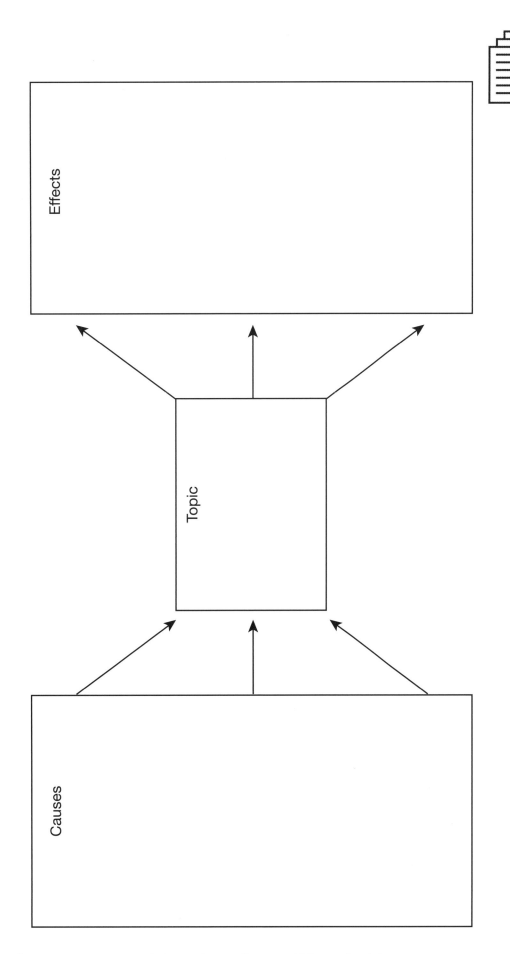

Causes

Topic

Effects

Cause and effect sorting cards

Cards to sort:

AUTUMN	The earth moves further away from the sun	The nights get longer
The earth tilts away from the sun	The days get shorter	The weather gets cooler
Animals get ready to hibernate	Some birds migrate to warmer countries	We wear warmer clothing

SUMMER	The earth moves closer to the sun	The nights get shorter
The earth tilts towards the sun	The days get longer	The weather gets warmer
Animals produce their young	Some birds migrate back from warmer countries	Risk of sunburn increases

PHOTOSYNTHESIS IN PLANTS	Oxygen is given out through the leaves	The nights get shorter
Sunlight falls on leaves	Food is made for the plant in the leaves	The plant grows
Water is taken in through the roots	Carbon dioxide is taken in through the leaves	

Torch story

Last weekend my friend Sam slept over. We stayed up very late playing. My Mum came into my room to tell us we had to go to sleep. It was dark, so Sam and I took my Dad's torch and played under the covers. I'm not sure when we finally fell asleep, but we left the torch on. In the morning, the batteries were flat and it did not work anymore. Yesterday, there was a big thunderstorm and there was a power cut. Dad went to get his torch so that we could see, but it didn't work. He wasn't very happy when he found out I had left it on all night and wasted the batteries. Now I have to help him to rake up all of the leaves that blew down in the storm!

We did not want to go to sleep	My friend Sam slept over	We played with the torch
We left the torch on over night	There was a power cut	There was a storm
Dad's torch did not work	I had to help clean up the leaves	

Sequence diagram

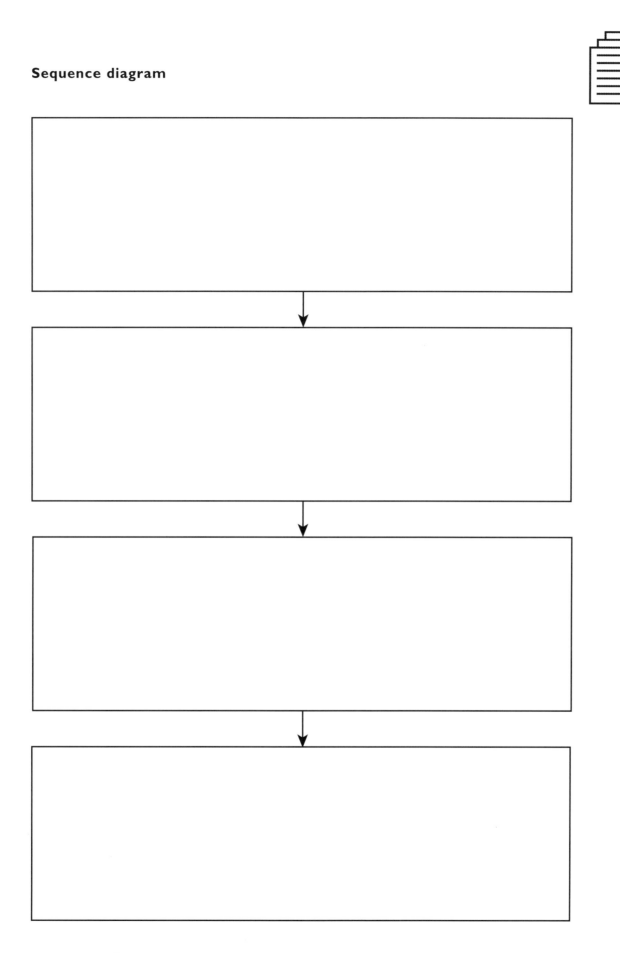

Venn diagram

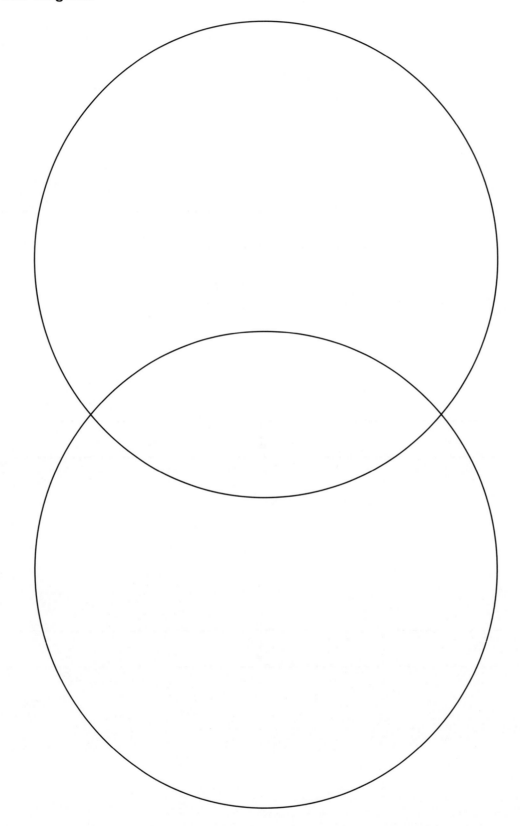

Football teams and their kits: label the Venn diagram circles blue and red

Arsenal Red	Everton Blue
Chelsea Blue	Man. City Blue
Liverpool Red	Blackburn Blue and Red

Animals: label the Venn diagram circles nocturnal and flying

Bat	Robin
Owl	Rabbit
Moth	Badger
Ostrich	Hedgehog
Butterfly	Wasp
Bee	Blackbird

What helps me to remember?

Stand on one foot	Concentrate
Make a picture in my head	Count the things to be remembered
Ask what was said	Say it over and over
Turn music on	Watch others to see what they are doing

What helps me to remember?

Look out of the window	Laugh
Play with my pencil	Link the things to be remembered together
Fiddle with my hair	Listen for the keywords
Trying to remember everything	Doing two things at the same time
Sing the things I want to remember to my favourite song	

Memory challenges

Someone rings and leaves a message for your brother, but your brother is not at home	You are in the queue for the ice cream van. Your two friends have told you what they would like you to buy for them
Your Mum asks you to go to the shop and get six things for her, but you do not have a shopping list	You are in the queue at the takeaway. Your friends are waiting outside and you have six things you need to remember to order
Your teacher has given you a list of five things that you need to do. It is important to do them in the right order	You want to phone your friend but do not have their number. You call another friend who gives you their number but you do not have a pencil to write it down
You are going on a school trip tomorrow and need to remember to bring a packed lunch	You have been invited to a party and need to remember to give your Mum the invitation when you get home
You got into trouble for not bringing your homework to school. You have done it but have left it at home. You need to remember to bring it tomorrow	You have a spelling test and have a list of 20 tricky spellings to learn
You have a times tables test	Your teacher has asked you to go to the stock cupboard and get some green paper, white paint, glue, rubbers and a pencil sharpener. How will you remember what to bring back?

Shape sorter challenge

Left   Top   Right

Bottom

Cut out the following shapes before starting the game

Cafe menu

Sausages	Cheese burger	Hamburger	Chips	Chicken nuggets
Peas	Baked beans	Chicken wrap	Pizza	Mushrooms
Fried egg	Fish fingers	Jacket potato	Spaghetti	Meatballs
Coffee	Milk	Coke	Tea	Orange juice

Sausages	Cheese burger	Hamburger	Chips	Chicken nuggets
Peas	Baked beans	Chicken wrap	Pizza	Mushrooms
Fried egg	Fish fingers	Jacket potato	Spaghetti	Meatballs
Coffee	Milk	Coke	Tea	Orange juice

Sausages	Cheese burger	Hamburger	Chips	Chicken nuggets
Peas	Baked beans	Chicken wrap	Pizza	Mushrooms
Fried egg	Fish fingers	Jacket potato	Spaghetti	Meatballs
Coffee	Milk	Coke	Tea	Orange juice

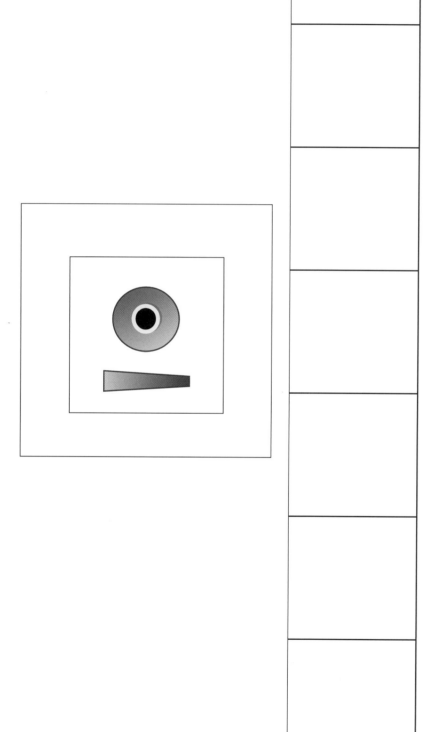

In the bag (at the beach)

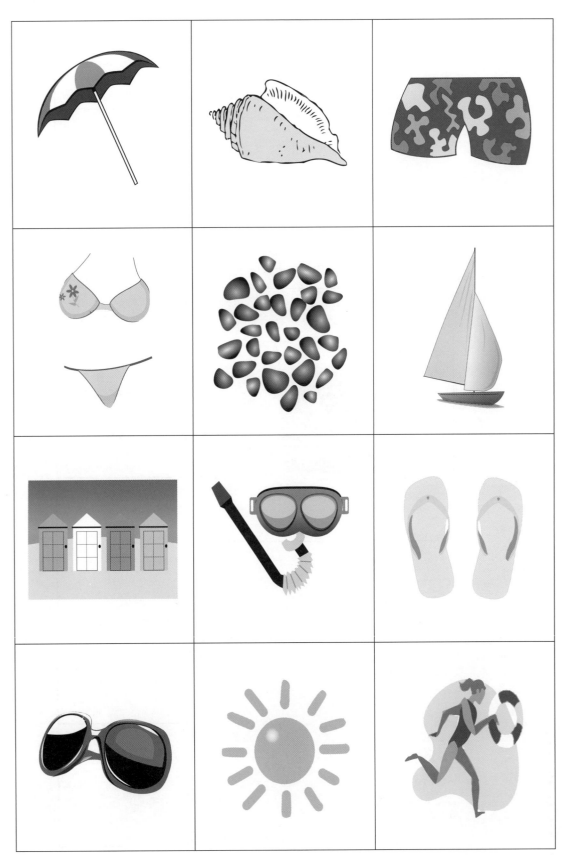

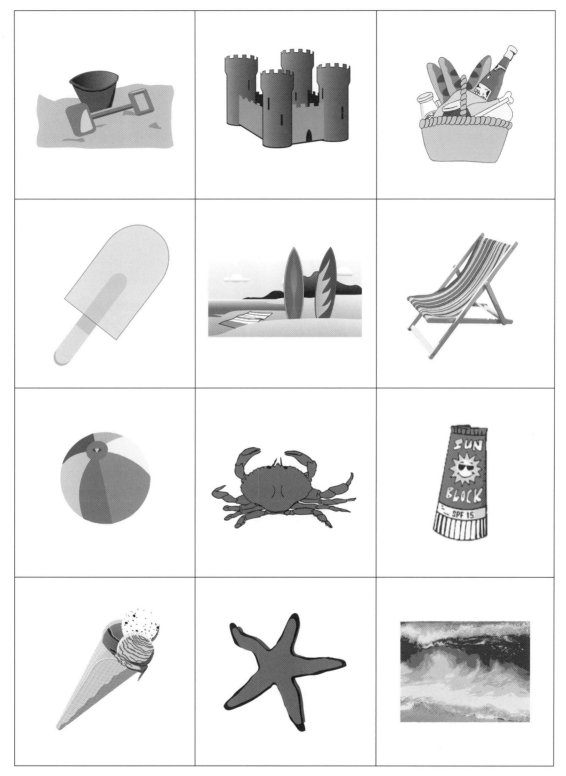

In the bag (at school)

In the bag (at the zoo)

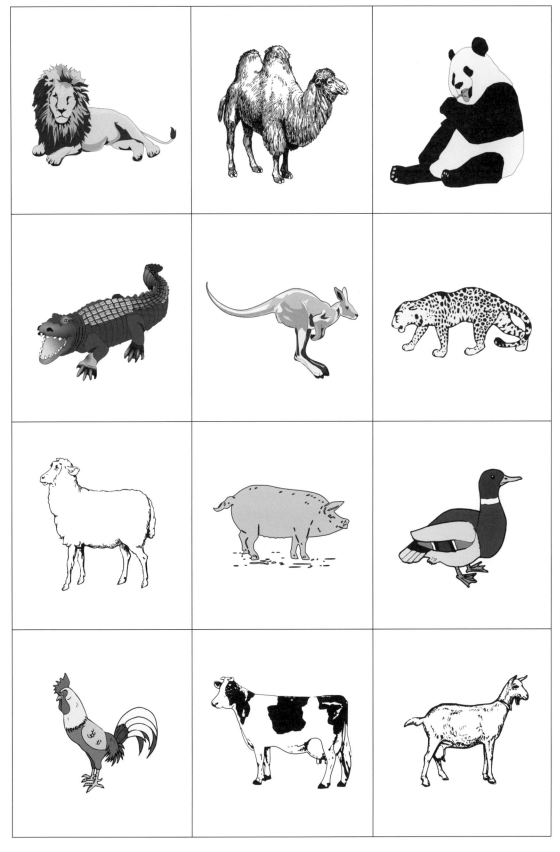

References

Alloway, T.P (2011) Improving Working Memory. Supporting Students' Learning. London. Sage.

Alloway, T.P (2009) 'Working memory but not IQ predicts subsequent learning in children with learning difficulties'. *European Journal of Psychological Assessment*, 25: 92–8.

Alloway, T.P., Gathercole, S.E., Kirkwood, H.J. and Elliot, J.E. (2009) 'The cognitive and behavioural characteristics of children with low working memory'. *Child Development*, 80: 606–21.

Cowan, N. and Alloway, T.P. (2008)'The development of working memory in childhood', in M. Courgae and N. Cowan (eds) *Development of Memory in Infancy and Childhood*, 2nd edition, pp. 303–42. Hove. Psychology Press.

Gathercole, S.E. and Alloway, T.P. (2008)Working Memory in the Classroom: A Practical Guide for Teachers. London. Sage.

Klingberg, T. (2009) The Overflowing Brain. Information Overload and the Limits of Working Memory. Oxford. Oxford University Press.

Swanson, H. Lee and Jerman, O. (2006) 'Math disabilities: a selective meta-analysis of the literature'. *Review of Educational Research*, 6 (2): 249–74.

Index

Activities and resources index